MEDITATION FOR MODERN MEN AND WOMEN

Ways of Prayer 6

Meditation for Modern Men and Women

Matthew McGetrick ODC

DOMINICAN PUBLICATIONS

First published (1983) by
Dominican Publications
St Saviour's
Dublin 1

© Matthew McGetrick ODC

ISBN 0 907271 20 0

Typeset and printed by
the Leinster Leader Ltd
Naas
Co Kildare

Acknowledgement

The Scripture quotations in this publication are from the Revised Standard Version of the Bible (Catholic Edition), copyrighted 1966 by the Division of Christian Education of the National Council of the Churches of Christ in the USA.

Contents

Introduction		1
1	Kinds of Meditation: The Mantra	6
2	Making Contact with the Ground of Our Being	14
3	Knowledge and Love	17
4	Desire for God	21
5	Relaxation	24
6	Virtue	31
7	Doing God's Will: Making Decisions	36
8	How to Cope with Suffering	40
9	How to Cope with Our Emotions	46
10	How to Cope with the Sex Instinct	50
11	The Cross of Christ	54
12	Humility	59
13	Conscience	63
14	Compunction of Heart	66
15	Freedom	69
16	Obedience	73
17	Christian Poverty	77
18	Harmony in Detail	79
19	The Light of Truth	82
20	Love	85
21	Auto-Suggestion	92
22	Making Sacrifices: Detachment	97
23	Effects on the Imagination and Body	102
24	Temptations	105
25	Dark Night of the Soul	108
26	A Goal in Life	112
27	Three Stages of Life	116
28	Perseverance	119
29	The Sacred Humanity of Christ in Contemplative Meditation	125
30	Our Invisible Friends	130
31	The Best Way to Help People	135

Acknowledgement

The Scripture quotations in this publications are from the Revised Standard Version of the Bible (Catholic Edition), copyrighted 1966 by the Division of Christian Education of the National Council of the Churches of Christ in the USA.

Introduction

The word "meditation" can be understood with different meanings. For many Christians it means reflecting on the life and teachings of Jesus Christ. For those who have learnt from oriental teachers it means cultivating a silent mind, empty of all thoughts. Such is Zen Buddhist meditation and transcendental meditation. But Christianity, too, has this silent meditation without thoughts, although it is not so well known. It is called contemplative meditation as distinct from the reflective kind which is known as discursive. It is also called infused prayer or mysticism or simply contemplation.

The word "contemplation" is sometimes used to indicate looking at a mental picture, as when we say "let us contemplate Christ as he preaches to the people on the mountain-side", but more usually it is used to denote the more mystical type of prayer without thoughts or mental pictures. It is in this latter sense I will use the word "contemplation". It is well to keep in mind that what the orientals call meditation is what we call contemplation, and I may often use either of these words with the same meaning.

There are two main kinds of contemplation, cosmic and Christian. Cosmic contemplation is an awareness of the underlying Being of the universe. Christian contemplation is an awareness of Christ in his work of redemption. The two can be separate or they can be united. Cosmic contemplation is within the capacity of human nature and can be attained by suitable training and technique, example TM; and some people have psychic powers which facilitate it. It is an experience of God in his creation, giving everything its being; an experience of universal Being underlying all particular beings; an experience of the oneness of all things, ourselves included; an experience of bliss and of love. And yet there is something impersonal about it. Even the love is impersonal. You are not aware that you are loving someone or that someone is loving you. Cosmic contemplation is something independent of historical events and is simply based on the relationship of particular beings to Universal Being. It tends to develop abstraction of mind in a person and to make it difficult for him to relate to the practical things of daily life. Hence some yogis take vows of lifelong silence, or have to be fed by their disciples so that their contemplation will not be interrupted.

Christian contemplation, on the other hand, is something that takes place within the setting of history, the history of salvation. It recognizes the reality of our call to share God's life, of our having lost it by sin, of our having been restored to it by the death and resurrection of Christ, of our incorporation with Christ in his Church, and of our receiving divine life through the visible rites of Mass and sacraments.

Non-Christian contemplatives would hold that this historical framework would injure the transcendental nature of contemplation (they use the word meditation where we say contemplation) because it is necessary to go beyond all concepts and images, that is, to transcend them, in order to make contact with the Ground and Source of Being. And even Christians often experience a certain perplexity as to whether they should occupy their minds in thinking about the history of salvation and conversing with Jesus our Saviour or try to transcend all such thoughts in order to make direct contact of will with the Source of Being.

The answer is simple enough: we should go to God with our whole nature according as he leads us. He must lead us. That is, we must try to make contact with him in the way that suits us best at any particular moment. We must follow the instinct of our souls through which he guides us and we must not make decisions based on our own ideas, that we are going to meditate one way or another. For example, it would be a great mistake if a person felt inclined to talk to Jesus and yet were to say to himself, "No, silent contemplation is more perfect, so I must make my mind a blank". On the other hand, if a person feels himself being drawn into a state of silent attentiveness he should give way to this attraction because, being a Christian, he is being drawn into union with Jesus at the level of pure spirit.

When I say that we should go to God with our whole nature I mean that there is a proper place for each manner of approach. There are times when we should study and reflect on the history of salvation and make it the basis of intimate conversation with Jesus. And it is often while we are engaged in such reflection and conversation that we shall feel ourselves drawn into an inner silence. This silence might last only a few moments and then we need to use our minds again in order to keep our attention directed towards God. As a rule, we should always give way to this call to inner silence and not force ourselves to continue whatever prayers we might have been saying. Sometimes this inner silence (St John of the Cross calls it a "loving attentiveness") becomes our normal state, interspersed perhaps here and there with simple thoughts or aspirations. But even in such cases we shall continue to nourish our thinking minds at other times by liturgical prayer and spiritual reading, or other devotions.

Transcendent contact with the infinite being of God is not injured by a contemplation which recognizes the sacred humanity of Jesus. Jesus as man is made up of a human soul as well as of a human body. We can use our imagination to think of him in his bodily form. Or we can allow ourselves to be drawn beyond thoughts and images into spiritual contact with his human soul. In either case we are in contact with his godhead, but in the latter case the contact is deeper and is beyond our power to produce at will. But always we are in Christ, whether through thoughts and images of him or through the silent contact of our spirit with his. In other words, when we are in a state of pure transcendence, our minds empty of all thoughts, we are still in Christ and through him in union with his godhead. But whereas cosmic meditators rely on techniques to produce transcendence, we rely on the grace of Christ that seeks to draw us ever deeper into himself; and, although we actively use our minds as much as is necessary to keep in touch with him, we are always ready to stop our thinking when we feel the call towards inner quietness.

I said that cosmic and Christian meditation can be separate or they can be united. A person without faith in God can enjoy cosmic meditation because to achieve it is within the power of our natural faculties. But should such a person receive the gift of faith in God, even without being Christian, such contemplation becomes supernatural, and divine life develops in his soul through Christ, even though through no fault of his own he might not believe in Christ. Among those who are Christian contemplatives it would seem that some enjoy cosmic contemplation as well, and some do not. St Francis of Assisi and St John of the Cross enjoyed cosmic contemplation, but there is no sign of it in St Teresa of Avila or St Therese of Lisieux. Merely appreciating the beauties of nature and praising God for them is not cosmic contemplation. But when cosmic contemplation exists in the life of a Christian contemplative, it is caught up into his Christian contemplation and is transformed by it. It ceases to be impersonal and becomes part of his personal intimacy with Christ. As St John of the Cross says, "My Beloved is the mountains, the solitary wooded valleys".

When we speak about contemplation we must bear in mind that we are talking about infused prayer or mystical contemplation. And when we think of mysticism we think of a kind of prayer that is the privilege of very few souls. It is true that they are comparatively few who reach the higher stages of mystical prayer, but there are initial stages of such prayer which seem very ordinary indeed and are open to anyone who knows how to dispose himself for them. God is only too willing to communicate with us and whenever he finds an opening he will come to us. When we speak to him he comes to us. When we work for him he comes to us. When we suffer for him he comes to us. When we open to him our intuitive minds he comes to us. This latter coming is initial contemplation. We can only do it at his invitation, but he is more ready to invite than we are to dispose ourselves. The intuitive mind is the silent mind, ignoring thoughts and images. When we thus turn to God he flows into us at a deep unconscious level and as a rule we have no feelings of any kind except attentiveness and peace. Yet this is mystical contemplation, the first simple stages of what reaches such sublime heights in saints.

It is generally thought that much reflection on the life and teachings of Jesus and much effort in the practice of virtue must take place before a soul is ready for contemplation. For high contemplation, yes, but for initial contemplation, no. All that is needed is a silent mind, directed towards God. Children can be very good contemplatives. They know how to look and to wonder without thinking. "I said my *mantra,* Jesus I love you! Then I got into silence. Then I lost it. Then I got into it again. I had one thought (i.e. distraction)." That from a child of eight. And she was not neglecting the practice of virtue: "I had a toothache but I said nothing about it. I offered it as a sacrifice to Jesus".

As children are subjected to the long process of education which in our culture concentrates almost entirely on developing the reasoning mind, their faculty for silent contemplation becomes submerged until they do not even know it exists and they are made to feel that having a silent mind is idleness and waste of time.

Now take the case of a person who at any stage of his life turns seriously to God for the first time but with very little knowledge of his religion. And suppose such a person feels attracted to remain before God with a silent mind. In fact God often gives this attraction at the very beginning of conversion. Through the light and love that comes in this silent attentiveness God will guide such a person gradually to do all that is required for the development of his spiritual life, to become familiar with the great mysteries of the life of Jesus, to see in himself the faults that have to be corrected and the virtues to be practised. It is contemplation that will guide his thinking mind in reflecting on the mysteries of faith and open his heart to live by the light of these mysteries. Our thinking mind is capable of attaining truth but without a guiding principle it can easily go astray. It can be misled by pride and prejudice and other selfish instincts. Even within the bounds of Christian orthodoxy there can be great confusion of opinions and this confusion is like a fog in the soul hindering progress. Contemplation is the guide. It gives an instinct for the truth and a desire to live by it.

According as the mind becomes more steeped in Christ, and one's whole being more transformed by his virtues so will contemplation take deeper possession of the soul and leave open the way for God to raise such a soul to whatever mystical heights he in his inscrutable design may plan for it.

1

Kinds of Meditation: The Mantra

I should like to say something now to help people to get started on contemplative meditation. Later on I shall describe the many wonderful effects it has on a person's life.

You should adopt a posture in which you can feel comfortable and relaxed but at the same time alert. Sitting in an easy chair is all right provided you do not go to sleep. Sitting on an upright chair is better. Using a meditation stool is better still. This is a stool about six inches high, sloping slightly forward, and eighteen inches long. You take off your shoes, kneel down on a carpet or mat, put the stool over your heels and sit back on it. This gives the body perfect balance and helps to keep the mind alert. It is quite comfortable, at least for half an hour, although some people prefer to have the stool a little higher than six inches. It is not desirable to do one's formal meditation in bed, but to meditate oneself to sleep is quite a different thing and there are many who find it helpful. Similarly, one can sometimes wake up in the early morning feeling rested and refreshed and find this an ideal time for meditating even while lying on in bed.

The body being thus comfortable and relaxed, the next thing is to relax the mind. We often begin a work of any kind by an anxiety to do it well and a fear that we might not do it well. This causes tension and puts an obstacle in the way of meditation. We must not think that we are going to something but rather that we are going to let something happen to us. We are going to let our mind quieten down and expose ourselves to an attraction that comes to us from a region beyond all thoughts and images. The trouble is that in the beginning this attraction is not strong enough to hold us and our mind will not stay quiet. So we have to make use of some technique to quieten our mind, which really means to quiten our imagination. Such techniques can be divided into two principal kinds, namely, discursive meditation and the mantra.

Discursive meditation on the life and teachings of Jesus Christ, apart from its intrinsic value, is also a technique for entry into contemplation. It presupposes you are a Christian, believing that Jesus Christ is God in human form. You choose any incident in his life, for example, when he lies asleep in the boat while the storm rages. Aroused by his terrified disciples, he stands and rebukes the storm and immediately there is a perfect calm. You see this picture in your mind and you look on yourself as being part of it. But you do not give all your attention to the storm or to the excited conversation of the disciples. You attention is focused on Jesus. How are you feeling about his being asleep while the storm rages? Do you want to wake him up, or do you trust him enough to believe that he has the whole situation in hand even though he sleeps? You talk to him, knowing that even in sleep he hears you.

Thus discursive meditation is neither a process of abstract thinking nor of creative imagination, although a certain amount of this latter is desirable. It is above all a means of making personal contact with Christ and of expressing our love for him in various ways. The essence of it is a loving conversation with Christ. However, this conversation gradually becomes simplified, even after a few minutes, and we are content to rest in the presence of Christ in an attitude of worship and love. This attitude is sustained by the repetition of a word or a phrase, such as: "With you I am safe," or "I trust you." Or any such words that hold us in an attitude of loving attentiveness to Christ. But the prayer is not so much in the words as in the attitude underlying them, and this might be an attitude of praise or of thanksgiving or of sorrow for sin or of petition for our needs, in fact any attitude which is suitable for a child of God in the presence of the heavenly Father, bearing in mind that Christ himself said, "He who has seen me has seen the Father". (John 14:9).

This is called the prayer of simplicity. It is a simplified form of discursive meditation because we are still occupied with thoughts although they are reduced to a very simplified form. Incidentally, it is well to bear in mind that all Christian meditation is prayer because it is not just a state of consciousness but also a loving attitude of the will towards God.

From this prayer of simplicity the transition to contemplative meditation is easy. It means passing from the state of being attentive to God with the help of a simple thought to the state of being attentive to him without any thought. Our mind has already become very quiet and we begin to feel the attraction of the Infinite. We no longer want thoughts about God, no matter how simple or inspiring; we want God himself. This means that God is drawing us into contemplation. Our part is gently to let go our thoughts and allow ourselves to be held by the attraction that comes from the Infinite. It seems like being attentive to nothing but in fact it is being attentive to him who is beyond all particular things. This is contemplation. When distractions come, as come they will, we gently fall back on our simple discursive prayer and at the same time keep ourselves in readiness to respond to any further call into this inner silence.

It is sometimes thought that one must spend considerable time in discursive meditation before venturing into contemplation, but this is not correct. A person can dispose himself for contemplation and feel the attraction towards it without ever having done any discursive meditation. Our intuitive power is part of our nature and whenever we open this power to God he communicates himself to it. The light we get in this contemplation will urge us to develop our thinking mind in discursive meditation if we have not already done so and will give us a deeper appreciation of the things we study, especially those things that relate to God.

For those who are not inclined to discursive meditation or the prayer of simplicity, entry into contemplation usually takes place by the use of a mantra. The word "mantra" is of Hindu origin but it describes something that has always existed in the Christian tradition though we never had a name for it. It usually refers to a word or a phrase that is repeated over and over silently in the mind, not in order to think about its meaning but to keep the imagination occupied and gradually quieten it, so that the will is not disturbed in its attention to the Infinite. The essence of contemplation lies in the attentiveness of our will to Infinite Being. As this is beyond the reach of our imagination the imagination remains unoccupied and restless and so needs to be given something to keep it quiet, and this is the purpose of the mantra.

A person begins meditation by relaxing body and mind, allowing the mind to be entirely loose and not focussing on anything. Naturally it will be flooded with distractions, and into this distracted state one gently introduces the mantra and keeps repeating it. You do not focus your attention on the mantra but rather you allow the mantra to attract your imagination to itself. The mantra has a certain silent vibration which has a magnetic effect on the imagination. That is why it is important that you should like the sound of the mantra, but you pay no attention to its meaning. Do not choose a mantra that is likely to set you thinking, yet it is desirable that it should have a meaning in some way connected with God or with Christ. The meaning gets into the unconscious mind and helps to direct the will towards the Infinite. For example, a phrase like "Come Lord Jesus", "In thee I trust", "My God and my All". But they do not need to have a definite religious meaning as long as they have what one might call a certain spiritual flavour. A phrase such as "Over the hills and far away" is quite a good mantra because it suggests infinity and going beyond all things. In fact the two words "Over" and "far" are in themselves good mantras. All the better if one needs only a single word. The quieter one's mind is the less one needs a mantra, and for a quiet mind a word is better than a phrase. Examples would be "God", "Love", "Holy", "Peace", "Amen", "Harmony" and "Tranquillity".

When you first introduce the mantra into your mind you keep on repeating it but you do not focus your mind on it. The focus of your attention by-passes it and goes straight out to the Infinite. It is as though the mantra were at one side of your mind. You can imagine it like this: think of the mantra as being on the right hand side of your mind and your imagination on the left hand side. The mantra is having a magnetic effect on your imagination, so that there is a horizontal line of magnetism between the two. Your will is in the centre and straight out in front is God, the Infinite. God is having a magnetic effect on your will so that between him and your will is a vertical line of magnetism. This is the essence of contemplation but in the beginning it is too weak to quieten the imagination and hold your attention. That is why the horizontal magnetism is needed, but as the vertical develops the horizontal gradually fades. In other words, the mantra gradually fades away as the attentiveness to God gets stronger.

Distractions are always likely to occur; and, when they do, one gently turns back again to the mantra, but no more than is necessary. It is a mistake to get upset about distractions or to start telling God you are sorry for them. That only brings you back onto the discursive level. It is best to turn back quietly and gently into the contemplative silence with the help of the mantra or even without it. If you start by using a phrase as a mantra it soon shrinks into a single word and even this fades into the background of your mind and might disappear entirely, to be brought back again only insofar as you might need it to keep away distractions. Contemplation is very pleasant when there are no distractions. It is then a state of pure consciousness or pure love, depending on whether you think of it in reference to the intellect or to the will. For "will" we can also use the word "heart" with the same meaning. By "heart" we do not mean the physical organ. It is a metaphor. But neither is it intended to suggest feelings of affection. It refers to the deep centre of our being, understood in a spiritual sense, and it implies a leaning and a longing of our being towards the object of our love. This is why contemplation is also called a prayer of the heart.

Distractions are of two kinds: those that interrupt the meditation and those that do not. The first kind are the real distractions and as soon as we are aware of them we turn back again to our meditation. The second kind are not really distractions. It is best to call them wandering thoughts. They would be distractions if we gave them our attention but we do not. We keep our attention on our meditation, while at the same time these wandering thoughts come and go in our imagination. There are two levels of activity in our mind at the same time. On the superficial level there is a continual flow of images that have nothing to do with meditation, while deep down our heart is being attentive to God.

The temptation here is to try to get rid of these wandering thoughts, and in doing so we only upset our meditation. We must not fight them but leave them alone, take no notice of them and keep our heart attentive to God. We must do our meditation along with these thoughts, ignoring them as best we can. The following illustration explains the attitude. A lady is entertaining a visitor in her sittingroom. In the room overhead her children are playing and making noise. If she goes up to quieten them they will be quiet for a few minutes and then be as bad as ever again, and meanwhile she has had to leave her visitor alone. So she decides to stay with her visitor and put up with the noise overhead. Thus we stay with God in meditation and put up with the noise in our imagination.

There are other things that can be used as mantras apart from words or phrases. If our mind is very active a mental picture will hold it better. A Christian will usually picture some scene from the life of Christ, for example the scene of Jesus talking to the Samaritan woman at the well of Jacob. And possibly repeating some words connected with it, such as, "I will give you living water". One must be careful not to start thinking about this scene, for that would be discursive meditation. Rather hold it to one side of the mind to keep the imagination occupied, while the attention of the heart goes out beyond it to the Infinite. As this attention gets stronger the picture gradually fades. Perhaps the words remain for a while and then these begin to fade, although sometimes one might have to use a mantra right through the period of meditation. A person sometimes thinks he is not meditating properly if the mantra does not fade away. This is not correct. Meditation is genuine even when one has to use the mantra all the time. It is better of course when it fades, but a person should be entirely satisfied with the kind of meditation he has here and now. Any anxiety to make it better will only spoil it.

A simple thought can also be used as a mantra, especially the thought of God. To think of yourself surrounded and penetrated by light which is God. To think of God as a great ocean into which you are plunging deeper and deeper. To think of the Spirit of Christ welling up within you and flooding your being. In fact these are images rather than thoughts and you do not allow your mind to think about them. You treat them exactly as you would a mantra.

Still another form of mantra is attentiveness to one's breathing. You do not try to breathe in any particular way but simply become aware of your breathing, and if you wish you can harmonize it with the repetition of a word or two. This, too, should be treated exactly like a mantra. There are people, though, who do not need any mantra or very seldom use one. They relax immediately into the nothingness which is really God. This could happen much oftener if people were not so much afraid to let go. They are afraid they might be doing nothing and are anxious to have some little image to cling on to. And so they cling on to a mantra instead of letting it go, and instead of being a help it becomes an obstacle. Contemplation lies in the attentiveness of the heart, and for that no thoughts or images or feelings are needed. St John of the Cross, that great Carmelite mystic and Doctor of the Church, describes contemplation as a loving attentiveness to God. If we want to go any further in describing it we have to use metaphors.

You can call it a looking of the soul towards God, a gaze of love. St John Mary Vianney, the Cure of Ars, noticed a man who spent a lot of time praying silently in church and one day he asked him how he prayed. The man, looking towards the tabernacle, said: "I look at him and he looks at me". That was contemplation. It can also be called a listening to God. The Bible tells us to listen to the voice of the Lord. "O that today you would harken to his voice! harden not your hearts." (Psalm 94:7-8). "Speak, Lord, for thy servant hears." (1 Samuel 3:9). Usually when we are listening we expect to hear something but in contemplation we must not expect to hear any words. God can and sometimes does speak to people in words, but their own unconscious minds can do the same and so can the evil spirit.

If you hear words in contemplation you should ignore them completely. If they are from God they will produce their effect without any interference from us, and if they are from ourselves or from the devil they can do us no harm if we ignore them. If the words contain a command for us to do something, we should consult a wise spiritual director and follow his advice. But as for the contemplation, as long as we remain in this attitude of listening, God is in fact communicating with us all the time but in a purely spiritual way in the unconscious region of our soul.

Contemplation can be thought of as waiting for God, but we do not expect him to come in any obvious way because as long as we remain in this attitude of waiting he is coming to us all the time in a way we cannot perceive.

Contemplation can also be described as a surrendering of ourselves to God. We like to be in control of situations that concern us. Even in prayer we like to be in control of our thoughts and of our conversation with God. But in contemplation we hand over to God and let him take control of what happens within us. We may feel as though our feet were being swept off the ground or as though we were being asked to jump over a precipice. Or we feel we have nothing to hold on to and we find ourselves instinctively groping for some little thing to hold on to, some little thought or image to make us feel that we really are in touch with God. Yet all this we must let go, and remain peacefully in the void, or allow ourselves to be swept off our feet, or jump recklessly over the precipice.

There are two basic psychological attitudes needed in contemplation: relaxation and focus. Relaxation removes the barriers caused by tension which prevent the free inflowing of God. But it is possible to be in a state of deep relaxation without thoughts or images and this might not be contemplation at all. In order that it be contemplation there must be focus on God. This does not mean focussing on some kind of thought or image of God. It means first of all having the general intention of doing meditation in order to get closer to God, and then during the actual meditation holding oneself in the emptiness, in the blankness of mind, paying no attention to any thought or image that might come, even thoughts or images of God. It is an attitude of refusing to give attention to anything because you want to be attentive to that which is beyond everything. It is an open-ended attentiveness, not focussed on anything but open to the Infinite. Even though it is an attraction coming from God that enables a person to have this attentiveness, nevertheless a person is usually aware of having to make an effort to hold himself attentive and to resist getting interested in thoughts or images that might come into his mind, even with a view to fighting and getting rid of them. However, there are times when the divine attraction is so strong that one has to make no effort whatever, and the time of meditation passes as though it were but a moment. When this is the case a person might easily think he has been asleep, yet he will come to realise that waking up from this kind of meditation is very different from waking up from sleep.

2

Making Contact with the Ground of Our Being

The purpose of Christian meditation is to achieve union with God. In no other way can we attain perfect and unending happiness. While this can be fully realised only in the life after death, we can go a long way towards it even here on earth, where meditation will give us, not only intimacy with God but many natural benefits as well which develop our personality and contribute to our success in life. All these fruits of meditation come from a single source which we can call Absolute Being, Universal Being, the Ground of Being, or simply Being Itself. And all these names mean God.

To say about something that it is a being is simply to say that it exists. But everything that goes to make up the world has only a limited existence. It exists according to its nature. The nature of a thing is like a box, capable of holding only a limited amount of existence. A horse has the existence of a horse and no more; a tree has the existence of a tree and no more; and so on with every created thing. But God does not have a nature that limits his existence; there is no box in him that can hold only a certain amount of existence. God's nature is existence itself. He is not this kind of being or that kind of being; he is Being Itself. This is why in contemplation we fix our attention on nothing in order to make immediate contact with him who is everything: Existence Itself, the Fulness of Being, the Infinite.

During the time of meditation we do not reflect on what we are doing. Such reflection would turn our attention away from the Infinite and fix it on our own state of mind, thus spoiling our meditation. But outside the time of meditation there are many things we need to reflect on in order to understand what meditation is all about and how to do it and what attitudes of mind we need to cultivate in order to allow it to develop. To supply such material for reflection is really the purpose of this book.

When we think of God as Absolute Being we think of ourselves and all created things as relative beings. This means that God depends on no one for his existence; he has it all in himself. But we and all created things depend for our existence on God. God made us out of nothing by an act of his will. Our body is part of the material of the universe, which itself was brought into existence out of sheer nothingness at the command of God. This took place at the beginning of time and at the beginning of the evolutionary process. But the soul of each human person is directly created by God at the moment when his life begins. And just as God drew us from nothingness by an act of creation, so he has to keep us in being by a continuance of this creative act. If he forgot about us for one moment we should fall back into nothingness again. You can close your eyes and form a mental picture of something. The moment you turn away your attention from it, it vanishes. We are like that in the presence of God. He has to keep holding us in being; left to ourselves we should vanish into nothingness. Our being is not our own, it is his. He gives it to us at each moment. Yet it is ours, too, because we are responsible for how we use it. We share in the being of God because we draw our being from him, but are not part of God because he is the Creator and we are his creatures. Having once created us God will never annihilate us. We are destined to live for ever, whether in happiness or in misery, depending on how we use our freedom, but this does not alter our condition of utter dependence on God. All prayer is based on a recognition of this dependence but this is particularly true of contemplative meditation, in which we play so small a part and God does so much.

We can also think of God as Universal Being and this means that he contains within himself the essence of all goodness and that therefore he is all-desirable. Goodness is just another aspect of being; it is the attractiveness that being has for our will. Whatever there is of goodness and beauty in any created thing exists also in God, but in so excellent and perfect a way that it is altogether beyond our power to imagine. St John of the Cross says that the beauty of this world is sheer ugliness in comparison with the beauty of God. And in fact nothing else can satisfy the human heart except the enjoyment of God. The reason is that since we can grasp the idea of unlimited happiness, we can never be satisfied with anything less. No matter how wonderful earthly happiness might be, sooner or later we come up against its limitations; we are dissatisfied and we want something more. Therefore, the only logical attitude is to make use of the good things of this world only insofar as they lead us to the infinite goodness of God. Our great problem is that we want to have our happiness immediately and so we cling to the good things of earth in a way that often holds us back from God. Contemplative meditation, by making us feel more deeply the attraction towards God, enables us also to see more clearly how to use earthly things in a way that leads to him.

God is also the ground of all being, like the soil out of which everything grows. Underlying everything we see, in fact, underlying everything that goes to make up the cosmos, there is a common element of being, something that gives unity to the whole of creation. It is God, who is present in everything he has made giving it its being. This is called the divine immanence, from the Latin words *"in manere"*, which mean "to remain in". It is balanced by what we call the divine transcendence, which means that God is also above and beyond everything. Hence it is deep in the centre of our being that we make direct contact with God, and yet we can only do this by going beyond everything that can be represented by a thought or image. In other words, we must transcend everything in order to make direct contact with him who is both immanent and transcendent.

3

Knowledge and Love

The chief faculties we use in our approach to God are our intellect and our will. All our faculties can help us; our imagination, our emotions, our bodily senses, but our intellect and will are of supreme importance. These are our spiritual faculties, they will exist in our soul after the death of our body. In themselves they are independent of matter, which is what is meant by saying they are spiritual and therefore they are capable of making direct contact with God who is the Supreme Spirit, entirely beyond matter. Although intellect and will always work in close harmony, their manner of operation is very different. The intellect takes in knowledge through ideas drawn from experience of the external world, whereas the will goes out to its object by desire or love. And because no idea can represent God as he really is, the intellect in this life cannot make direct contact with God but only with ideas about him. In heaven the intellect will grasp God directly and not an idea of him, and this is known as the beatific vision.

The will, however, can make direct contact with God even here on earth because it does not take its object into itself, thus limiting it, but rather goes out to its object and contacts it as it is in itself. Thus when we desire or love God it is God himself we desire or love and not just an idea of him. Therefore in our service of God here on earth the will is more important than the intellect, although both are necessary.

The function of the intellect is to inspire the will to love God. Or instead of the words 'intellect' and 'will' we can use the words 'mind' and 'heart' with the same meaning. We cannot love what we do not know, and the more we get to know about someone who is really good, the more we love him. Whatever knowledge we get about any of the arts or sciences simply means discovering something that God has put into his universe. When we think of the great advances in medicine, and of how our lives have been changed by the use of railways, motorcars, telephone, television and innumerable modern conveniences, do we realise that we have been discovering things that God has made and put into his universe, and that they were there all the time awaiting our discovery? They provide so many new reasons for praising the power and wisdom of God and loving him all the more. The same is true of the life of a student. Whether it be physics, chemistry, biology, history, sculpture or literature, or any other branch of study or skill, he is getting to know things that God has made and is discovering new reasons for loving him more. Thus all activity of the intellect should inspire the will to love God.

Unfortunately, the very opposite is what often happens. Only too often intellectual activity leads a person away from God. The basic reason for this is the way the intellect itself operates, namely, by taking in ideas. As a person's knowledge increases he feels his mind is growing. He comes to know things that many others do not know and can do things that many others are not able to do. This gives him a feeling of self-sufficiency and independence. Of course there is nothing wrong about being as self-sufficient as possible provided a person uses his power in the service of others and especially of God. But to be complacent about one's powers, using them merely for one's own enjoyment and advantage, turns a person in upon himself and separates him from other people and from God. It is the vice of pride, the greatest obstacle to union with God.

This attachment to intellectual activity for the sake of the pleasure and advantage it affords can hold a person back from God even in matters spiritual and religious. The study of theology, of the Bible, of Church history, and even of prayer itself and the spiritual life, all this can remain at the level of intellect without inspiring the will, can be done for the sake of the natural satisfaction of the study involved, and can even develop pride, as is sometimes evident when a scholar who considers himself a specialist on a subject finds his opinions being criticised by others.

I heard of a professor of dogmatic theology in a Roman seminary many years ago, who was absolutely orthodox in his teaching, and yet had no faith. He did not believe what he taught but taught it correctly in order to earn his living. That is an extreme case, but there are many who teach the way of Christ and have a good intention in doing so, but are more concerned with helping others than with practising it themselves. The danger is that not being illuminated by the Spirit of Christ they will make subtle mistakes that they may not even be aware of, and lead others astray. Like those in authority, those also who teach Christianity have a special obligation to live under the influence of the Holy Spirit.

It is important, then, to know how to use our intellect in spiritual matters so that it will lead us closer to God in love. First of all, if we are Christians, it is necessary to have a basic knowledge of the teachings of Christ as proclaimed by his Church. It is not enough to draw this teaching directly from the Bible itself. It is too easy to interpret things to suit outselves and to ignore what we do not like. Christ told his Church to teach, and the Church presents us with this teaching as through the course of centuries it has come to be expressed in clearer and more precise terms, and shows us how to apply it to the varying circumstances of human life. Apart from sermons and lectures there are many excellent books available to help us to live a truly spiritual life as Christians.

The next step is to make this knowledge personal by talking to Jesus Christ about it. This is what happens in discursive meditation, which can also take the form of meditative reading. We read a spiritual book in the presence of Jesus, turning to him frequently as we read, with thoughts of praise or thanksgiving or sorrow for sin, or asking for his help in understanding what we read and in putting it in practice in our lives. In fact we become more interested in the personal contact with Jesus than in the actual thoughts which led us to this. All study of religious subjects should be coloured by this personal element, which will save us from falling back into mere intellectualism and will direct our hearts towards love.

The highest use of our intellect is, in a sense, not to use it at all but allow it to be used by God. This is what happens in contemplative meditation. Our activity passes from the intellect to the will. The will is occupied in a calm attentiveness to the Infinite. Sometimes an effort is required to hold it in this state against the pull of distractions. At other times it is so held by God that no effort is needed and one is not even aware of the passage of time. Meanwhile the intellect is at rest, but receptive and highly sensitive. It is in an intuitive state. We refer to it as the intuitive mind, as distinct from the ordinary thinking mind. It is like the calm water of a lake which reflects clearly the images of trees by the shore, or like a sensitive photographic plate which receives the clear imprint of a picture.

In this state of silent mind and attentiveness of will a contact with God is established which can be compared to a pipeline through which God flows into the soul, not only increasing love in the will but also giving spiritual light to the mind. The mind or intellect is here at its highest level of perfection because it is not depending on its own activity but is being enlightened by God. This enlightenment has remarkable effects, not only in the appreciation of spiritual realities but also in the practical affairs of daily life, as I shall explain when I come to speak of the light of truth.

4

Desire for God

Since will-contact is the essential condition for contemplation, it is important to develop it as fully as possible. Of course it is God himself who develops it by attracting our hearts to himself, but there is something we can do to help the process and we must try to do all we can. We must have a clear conviction, and often remind ourselves of it, that God is all-desirable. One might well wonder why it is, if God is all-desirable as he certainly is, that everyone does not run to him as to a dearest friend and lover. In fact the opposite is more frequently the case.

People run away from God. And even those people who have enough faith to want to keep in with him, only too often have no desire to get close to him. The reason is, of course, that God is holy and we are sinful. God is spotlessly pure and beautiful and we are spiritually dirty and disfigured. Therefore we are afraid to come close to God, feeling sure he would punish us. and while we tell ourselves that God is a loving Father, we still want to keep at a distance from him and hope he will make everything all right. The simple fact is, however, that sooner or later we shall have to end up either happy with God or eternally miserable without him. And the only logical thing to do is to keep moving in the direction of happiness. God is not out to punish us. He wants to heal our spiritual wounds, to cleanse our hearts of evil. He supports and helps us in this process, sweetening by his love whatever pain may be involved, and giving us wonderful foretastes of the happiness he has in store for us when we are ready for it, even in this life, to say nothing of the unimaginable happiness of being with him after death.

We have good reason, then, to come close to God, even though in the beginning we may feel ashamed in his presence, because gradually and with love he will change us and make us like himself and then our happiness will be complete.

The story of the life of Jesus as told in the gospels, is full of this message. Jesus is God in human form and he is saying to us, "Do not be afraid, come to me and I will make everything right for you." But unfortunately many people say to themselves, "I do not really want to get close to you, Lord, but please make everything right anyway." Impossible wish!

It is impossible for us to imagine how greatly God desires to win our hearts. He has nothing to gain from us yet he loves us because he made us; and he is always trying to enkindle in our hearts a desire for him, for he cannot come to us unless we are willing to receive him. Such is the mystery of free-will, we are free to choose happiness or misery. The more we desire him the more he can give us a share in his life and fill us with his presence in contemplation. Desire increases our capacity to receive. Metaphorically speaking, we can say that it opens out within us a yawning chasm that cries out to be filled. In the life of Jesus we see God reaching down to us to touch our hearts with a longing for him so that he might give himself to us more completely.

Think of the charm of Christmas, how it has captivated people's hearts as they contemplate God lying as a baby in a manger. It is as though he were saying, "Fear not to come to me; see, I have become very small and weak". And every year people are touched by the spiritual charm of Christmas; they experience a new turning of their lives to God. No matter where we contemplate Jesus in his earthly life we find him attractive. The crowds flocked around him wherever he went. They would forget to eat in order to listen to his words. "Never did man speak like this man", they said. And this is the God whom nowadays people are afraid of and do not want to get close to and do not want to believe in!

True, when it came to his arrest and torture the crowds fell away from him; even his disciples were scattered. He had to show us that we are sinners and that the sufferings of life are the price of sin. But then he did what no one else has ever done: he came back to life again by his own power, with a body that could no longer suffer; gathered his disciples together once more and assured them that if they went through the troubles of life in spiritual union with him, they too would rise to a new life and would suffer no more. Everywhere the message of the gospel is the same: we brought misfortune on ourselves by sin, but God has come to heal our wounds, to comfort us in our troubles and to lead us to endless life and happiness. Why, then, are we afraid of drawing close to God? It is of losing him we ought to be afraid.

While philosophical reflection and discursive meditation on the life of Jesus give us considerable help in cultivating a desire for God, they do not go far enough. They are important because God will not help us unless we help ourselves. We must do all we can, however little it might be, and then God will do everything that is needed, even if it means working miracles for us. It is in contemplation that God takes pity on our puny efforts and enkindles in our hearts a great longing or desire for him. Contemplation of its very nature develops this desire in us. It puts us in contact with Infinite Being and we are attracted by its goodness; goodness is simply the attractiveness of being. There is what we might call a magnetic power coming from the Source of Being and attracting all beings to itself, and we expose ourselves fully to this influence when we go beyond all our thoughts and feelings.

But there is more than this impersonal attraction between Creator and creature. There is the personal invitation of a Father to this children, inviting them to come and share his own life. That is something we could never have dreamt of if God had not given it to us. As human beings we could merit human happiness, the bliss of enjoying a perfect world with the glory of the Creator shining through it, but he himself would be infinitely beyond our range of vision. That would be our natural destiny as human beings. But God did not leave us like that. He decided to admit us to the enjoyment of his own personal life, to give us a divine happiness which would include human happiness and go far beyond it.

This is what we call supernatural life because it is beyond the power of our own nature. It comes to us with the gift of faith and is developed through loving service of God. In this life we develop it without seeing it. After death we enjoy to the full what we have developed. There is a great longing in the heart of our heavenly Father to draw us into the happiness that he himself enjoys, and we fully open our souls to this attraction in contemplative meditation.

5

Relaxation

While the attentiveness of our heart to God is of the very essence of contemplation, there is a natural state of mind which is highly important for its success, and that is the state of relaxation. Relaxation loosens our body, calms our nervous system and gives peace to our mind so that our vital energy can flow freely for the doing of whatever work we are engaged on. A baseball coach has said that if a player is tense he plays a bad game, but if he is relaxed his energy flows in an easy rhythm and he plays well. I knew a priest who was very anxious to give a good sermon on our Lady, so anxious that he became tense and gave a bad one. And there was a girl who wanted to be an air hostess but when she came to an interview she got so tense that she became tongue-tied and could say nothing. Having failed with five different companies she became reckless and tried once again, not caring what she said, and had no difficulty in getting the job.

Just as relaxation enables our own energy to flow out from us freely, so also it enables God's energy to flow into us freely. It is true that God can give grace and even very powerful grace to a person who is tense and emotionally upset, especially when such a person calls out to him from the depth of his heart with humility and trust, but there is something special about the work God does in a soul through contemplation, which requires that the person be very relaxed, peaceful and receptive. St John of the Cross speaks of this inflowing of God through contemplation as a delicate anointing of the soul, and because it is so delicate, refined and penetrating the person receiving it needs to be entirely at rest so as not to impede the divine action by any tension or activity of its own. In fact it is God himself who gives the relaxation that is necessary. We can only go a little way towards acquiring it, but we must never forget the principle that it is only when we do all we can that God does all that is needed. So let us take a look at our lives and see to what extent we are subject to tension.

It would seem that many people suffer from excessive pressure of work, and they have even come to look upon this condition as a normal part of life so that they do not realise the injury it is doing them nor feel the need of finding a remedy for it. It is right that a person should work to the full limit of his capacity; that gives him a sense of peace and fulfilment. But to work beyond one's capacity causes strain and anxiety.

If a person is giving God the top priority in his life he will seek a job that suits him, not necessarily the job that brings in the most money, and he will even be satisfied with a lower standard of living for himself and his family rather than overwork himself. Many husbands think they are acting nobly by overworking themselves to provide more money for their families, when their families would prefer to have more of their loving presence in the home. Ambition or the desire for money leads people to do more than they are able to do. This produces nervous strain and anxiety which lowers their vitality and injures the quality of all their work and may eventually lead to a nervous breakdown.

But there are other more worthy motives which lead people to undertake too much, and because the motives are so good they do not realise that they are making a mistake. It may be a case of doing voluntary good work for the welfare of other people, for the disabled, the elderly, the poor. And it is very desirable indeed that there should be people to do these works. But one should never forget the principle: never work beyond your capacity. If you do, everything suffers.

The thing that suffers most of all is one's life of prayer. You are so busy helping people that often you have no time to meditate. You excuse yourself by saying that you find Christ in people. But Christ also said that we should go into our room and close the door upon us and pray to our Father in secret. During his public life Christ gave himself unreservedly to people. They crowded in upon him so much that he had scarcely time to eat. But when darkness came and the people went home to sleep he would go out into the lonely mountains and spend whole nights in prayer. If we cannot spend nights in prayer we must at least find time for it during the day. There is a time for meeting Christ in people and there is also a time for meeting him in the intimacy of prayer. He has a right to that and he wants it.

The practical question we need to ask ourselves is: if we are too busy to find time for meditation, or if, when we do, we are too tired to be able to do it properly, how are we going to remedy this situation? It is true that there are certain duties that we cannot change even if they seem to be too much for us, and therefore we accept them as God's will for us. We accept them without complaint, with a joyful spirit, leaning upon the help of God, knowing that even if they do cause us some injury he will turn it to greater good. But there are other things which it is in our power to control. We can resign from certain societies or committees, give up certain friendships that absorb too much of our time, and not be afraid to say No when people ask us to do things. Some people think they would be refusing God if they refused a request to take on a good work in his service. But if it meant having to work beyond our capacity it is certainly not God who is asking us.

I heard of a priest many years ago in Ireland who had a great reputation as a marriage counsellor. People flocked to him from all over the country, and because their need was so great and he felt he could help them, he could not bring himself to say No to any request, with the result that he worked himself into a serious nervous breakdown. He had to give up all his work and go to Australia to get away from it all. How much more would he have been able to help people had he known how to keep his work within the limits of his capacity.

Granted that we do what we can to relieve the external pressures in our life we must also do what we can to develop a relaxed attitude of mind and body. Even in a busy life there will be a moments when one has nothing special to do. These are the times to practise relaxation. In some places classes are given in relaxation and it is often taught in yoga classes, but one can always do a little on one's own. When you have a few moments to spare do not start looking for something to do like taking up a paper or magazine or turning on the radio or television. Instead, practise relaxation. However, there is a certain difficulty about how to begin.

Anything else you do requires that you make an effort to do it, but if you make an effort to relax you become more tense, because relaxation means the letting go of effort. Some teachers advise deliberately tensing your muscles and then letting go in order to experience the feeling of relaxation, but personally I prefer the method of auto-suggestion. It works like this, and I am presuming that a person can only devote a few minutes to the practise at any given time.

Sit in a comfortable chair, close your eyes and rest your hands on your lap. The hands are important because so much of the work we do is done with our hands; the tension shows itself in them as one notices when people make fidgety movements with their fingers. So with your eyes closed you focus your mind on your hands and talk to yourself about them."I relax my hands, my hands are relaxing, my hands are completely relaxed". You say these words slowly and quietly, and the very use of the word "relax" tends to produce the effect of relaxation in your hands. This is auto-suggestion. You are suggesting relaxation to yourself, in particular to your hands.

Another part of the body where tension often shows itself is the forehead, especially the tension caused by worry and anxiety. You go through the same process here, with your eyes closed and your mind gently focused on forehead. You can also take in your whole body at a glance, and either repeat the words as given above, "I relax my body, etc." or other words that suggest relaxation, "My body is limp, heavy, sinking, loosening out, falling to pieces'; but use only one such expression at a time, repeating it slowly, and pausing after each repetition.

So much for general exercises in relaxation, with which we can occupy our spare moments at any time. But there is also what we call conditioned relaxation which means developing a relaxed attitude towards certain situations which we foresee are likely to be tension-producing. Suppose you will be having an interview with someone tomorrow which you foresee is likely to be unpleasant. There is some difficult business to be done and angry feelings are likely to be aroused. The very thought of the meeting upsets you and makes you feel anxious and tense.

To develop a relaxed attitude you remind yourself that every situation has a positive and a negative side. On the negative side, fear grips your imagination so that it unduly magnifies the unpleasantness of the situation. You recognize this tendency and deliberately play down what your imagination builds up. You tell yourself that things will not be nearly as bad as you fear because your imagination is making you see things in a false light.

Then you decide that you will develop a positive attitude towards the situation, which means that you will meet the person with an attitude of good will. You will listen to what he says, try to understand his point of view, show sympathy for his difficulties and even be prepared to give in to him as far as would be reasonable. Then if you feel in duty bound to take a stand on certain points, while you must indeed be firm and unyielding, you nevertheless express yourself with gentleness, explaining your reasons, and even being apologetic for having to seem so unrelenting. When a harsh truth is expressed with love for the person you are speaking to, he is more likely to accept it and may even come to look on you as his friend. But even if he does not take it well and is angry with you, you at least will remain patient, not resenting his anger and not losing your peace of mind. When you have learnt from experience how this approach proves successful, you will gain confidence in it and it will work all the better.

All these methods of relaxation which I have suggested are really only dealing with the symptoms of tension. They give temporary relief but they do not cure the tension at its roots. To bring about this cure the grace of God is needed and especially the virtue of trust. The reason we worry and get tense is that we feel it is up to us to solve our problems and we do not know how to do it. We need to hand over our lives to God so that he can control and direct them his own way. This relieves us of worry and relaxes our tensions. As the Bible says, "Cast your burden upon the Lord and he will sustain you." Ps 55:22). An illustration will explain what I mean.

Imagine an elderly lady who lives alone in a large house with beautiful grounds. She is wealthy and has everything she needs, but her money is tied up in mysterious ways that she does not understand and she lives in constant fear that there will be some crisis in the financial world and she will lose everything. This fear takes all the pleasure out of her life, so that her wealth brings her no happiness. Then it happens that a man comes back into her life whom she had known many years previously and who had been a trusted friend. She knew him to be an expert in financial matters and she tells him all about her fears. His comment is, "I understand the situation thoroughly. Leave the matter in my hands and I assure you everything will be put right. It will take some time, so keep in touch ith me and do what I tell you. You may need to see a solicitor from time to time and sign certain documents, but I will tell you exactly what to do and when to do it. Keep in touch with me and I can promise you that all will be well." From that moment the burden of fear is lifted and the old lady worries no more. Because she trusts her friend completely she knows that everything will be all right and as far as she is concerned everything is all right from now. She is only too happy to do whatever he tells her.

This expresses the attitude we should have towards God. We should leave all the affairs of our life in his hands, keep in touch with him and do what he tells us. Then we should have nothing to worry about and no cause for tension. To many people this would seem idealistic and impossible. "Will God pay my bills for me", one might ask. And the answer is, "Yes, God will get into your mind and work through your mind in everything you do". It will seem that it is you who are doing things but it is really God in you who is doing them. You are aware of this and so you have perfect peace.

The big question is, how does one acquire this trust. It is easy to say, "Lord I trust you" and then go on worrying as though we had never said it. Words are not enough, our trust must be real. To achieve this takes time and effort. We must treat worry as we would treat a temptation to sin: we must never allow ourselves to think on it deliberately. Whenever a worry comes to mind we must give it to God and leave it to him. By worry I mean thinking to no purpose, when our mind keeps going round in circles and sees no answer to our problem. When we find ourselves doing that we must turn it to God every time and forget about it. We must keep doing this continually, even a hundred times a day or more, until gradually we develop the habit of leaving our problems with God.

You might say that you must think about your problems in order to solve them. True, there is practical thinking which is directed towards investigating the facts of a situation and weighing them up in order to make a decision. That is good. But when one has done the practical thinking on a matter and yet there is no solution in sight and the mind keeps endlessly brooding on the problem, that is worry. That is what must be given to God. God is very pleased with this continual effort on our part to sacrifice our worries to him, and sometimes gradually, sometimes suddenly, he takes over our life. But to persevere in this effort is in itself a problem. People forget so easily in spite of their good intentions, and allow themselves to get caught up in their worries.

What is needed is the spiritual awareness that comes with contemplative meditation. Good resolutions are not enough. Even praying for God's help in discursive meditation is not enough. It has its own value, but it does not go far enough. Contemplative meditation makes a person alert to every opportunity of sacrificing worry to God, and it also disposes a person to receive the spiritual light by which he will be guided in solving his problems. To keep in touch with God and to do what he tells us is accomplished through contemplative meditation. He does not speak to us by words or by signs but he works within our mind, enabling us to do the right thing at the right time and always to remain at peace.

When this perfect trust in God has become a reality a great

change takes place in a person's life. He is lifted out of the narrow groove of a self-centred individual life and becomes part of a cosmic life-stream which is flowing on towards the eternal kingdom of Christ. Here on earth God is preparing the future citizens for the places they will eventually take in his kingdom. Even among those who allow him to work in them, his work is hampered because they do not surrender themselves to him but at least to some extent keep wanting to have things their own way.

When a person finally surrenders his life to God completely then God is free to work his will to the full, and such a person is caught up into a world-wide plan by which the kingdom of heaven is being prepared on earth. This gives him a wonderful feeling of freedom and security and a peace of soul that nothing can disturb. This is the complete answer to the problem of tension and relaxation. While relaxation is an important disposition for contemplation, it is contemplation itself which gives perfect relaxation. A gentle, persevering effort is required of us all along the way, but is God himself who gives the result.

6

Virtue

So far I have been speaking chiefly about contemplation itself and ways in which we can dispose our minds to receive it, but from now I shall have a lot to say about the receptacle into which contemplation flows. I call it the soul, and it includes the whole of our psychic life; our mind and heart, our emotions and instincts, and even our body inasmuch as this too is animated by the soul.

God flows into us in contemplation, communicating his light and his love, but there are obstacles within us which prevent him from taking full possession of us. Many of our attitudes are disordered, that is to say, not in accordance with the requirements of reality, as, for example, when we have an attitude of ill-will towards a person instead of good-will. There can be many such disorders within us and they offer barriers to the inflowing of God. Imagine the soul as having a number of channels linking up every part of it, like arteries and veins in the body. God wishes to flow through all these channels in order to enter into every part of the soul, but in many places they are twisted and knotted so that he cannot get through. What this means in reality is that when we have a habit of reacting the wrong way in any situation we are offering an obstacle to the inflowing of God. In other words, we are lacking in virtue; so in order to be completely open to God we need to develop all the virtues.

Any one who has been educated as a Christian has a fair idea of the basic Christian virtues: faith, hope, love of God and of people, humility, patience, courage, justice, chastity and so on. But all virtues have something in common, namely, harmony. Virtue can be described as a deep-rooted attitude of heart which inclines a person to react in a harmonious way in any given situation. God created the world as a thing of order and harmony and he gave it laws to ensure that it would function in a harmonious way. These laws govern the movements of the heavenly bodies and the behaviour of all living things. They govern the behaviour of man too except that man has the privilege of freely submitting to them so that he may express his love for the Creator and merit a reward. But freedom gives him the power to act against the divinely-planned order, and his sinful inclinations often lead him to do this. These disorderly inclinations are overcome by the development of contrary inclinations or habits which urge him to act according to the harmony of God's law. These good inclinations are called virtues.

Take for example the virtue of faith. Faith means taking God's word for something. God speaks to us through Jesus Christ and through his Church. Once we recognize this, the only harmonious reaction is to listen and to obey. To refuse to listen to God and to obey him when he speaks would be a disorder. Or take the virtue of courage. You have a painful duty to accomplish and your inclination is to run from it, but you know that the right thing is to face up to it and do it. This is the reaction that is required by the reality of the situation. It is the harmonious reaction; in this case the virtue of courage.

Virtue is the source of many benefits. First of all it brings interior peace. Our disordered reactions cause us a lot of trouble and upset. Impatience, jealousy, resentment and many other such disordered reactions bring much misery into our lives. When these are transformed into virtuous reactions great inner peace is the result. Virtue also enables us to do our work better, whatever it might be, because the vital energy that had been consumed by disorderly reactions is now free to be directed towards our work. A further benefit is that virtue greatly improves our relationships with other people. They feel the harmony that comes from us and they are attracted by it. People like us and we find it easy to get on with them. However, it would be a great mistake to develop virtue merely for the sake of these practical advantages. Such an effort would be ego-centred and would lead to one of the greatest of disorders, the vice of pride.

We should develop virtue in order to open up our soul to the inflowing of God, so that he can enter in and take possession of us in an intimate love-relationship. We need not be afraid that we might lose our individuality and our freedom by such intimacy. It is God who gives us everything we have and we are never more truly ourselves than when we are fully under his control.

We practise virtue, then, in order to make way for contemplation. It can be said that the spiritual life develops along parallel lines, the line of prayer (and this includes especially contemplative meditation) and the line of virtue. Contemplation enables a person to develop in virtue and virtue opens the way for deeper contemplation. It would be highly dangerous for a person to practise contemplation without at the same time trying to practise virtue. He would be opening his soul to the inflowing of God and at the same time not allowing him to enter. The result would be that other forces would begin to operate, namely, his own unconscious mind and evil spirit. He would develop a desire for interesting experiences and these forces would supply them. He might hear words which he would think came from God, or see interior visions with wonderful meaning, or receive a call to do some great work in the world, or to go to other people and tell them what is wrong with them. In a word, he would come to see himself as someone specially chosen by God and would feel very proud of it, whereas in reality he would have drifted away from God and be at the mercy of his own unconscious ambitions, stimulated and intensified by the evil spirit.

Virtue not only opens the soul to the inflowing of God but it also strengthens it to be able to take this inflowing in all its power. Although God flows in silently and deeply he can come very powerfully, and it is a virtue that gives the soul a balance and a strength to be able to take this inflowing without breaking down beneath it. Otherwise it would be like a heavy man sitting on a fragile stool that collapses beneath him.

However, a person should avoid the opposite mistake of thinking that he must acquire considerable virtue before he even begins to contemplate. In fact one cannot acquire virtue without the help of prayer, and God often gives contemplation even at the very beginning of one's spiritual life, even after one has only just turned away from serious sin. This does not mean that such persons are suddenly advanced in holiness or that they should neglect to read and reflect on spiritual truths, but it means that God is giving them contemplation to give them a good start in the spiritual life, and they should accept it with gratitude and follow the light it gives. All that is needed is that contemplation and virtue should develop together and then a person need have no fear of going astray.

Now we come to the practical question of how to develop virtue. People are sometimes advised to concentrate on practising one virtue at a time, say over a period of a month, and then passing on to another, keeping note from day to day of their failures, which hopefully should be fewer as the days pass. Anyone who finds this method helpful should certainly make use of it, but for most people it ould seem rather unrealistic and artificial.

An intellectual knowledge of the virtues is gained through spiritual reading. Almost any spiritual book will have something to tell us about virtues even though it does not give them the label of their titles. Then by prayerful conversation with Christ we direct this knowledge towards practice. But it is only when this discursive meditation develops into contemplation that the urge towards virtue becomes strong. But it must be remembered that contemplation can often be intermingled with quite a deep form of discursive meditation.

The light that comes through contemplation throws a spotlight on a particular fault that God wants us to correct, and it is not so much an external fault as an inner attitude of heart that is in question. If the attitude of heart is corrected the corresponding external behaviour soon comes right. God does not tell us in general that we need a certain virtue but he shows us a particular fault to be corrected. It is for us then to decide what the right reaction would be in that situation, in other words, what would be the Christlike way of reacting. Contemplation will also give us light to see this, because our own thinking might easily be mistaken. And furthermore, we must see this right reaction as something altogether attractive and desirable, something that we really want in spite of possible selfish inclinations to the contrary.

We can be certain that all virtue is desirable because all virtue is harmony. We form a mental picture of ourselves reacting the right way to the situation in which formerly we were at fault. We frequently hold this picture before our mind together with a prayerful desire that God would make it a reality in our conduct. In this way we are carving out a new groove in our mind. The reason why people keep committing the same fault in spite of their desire to change is that the faults have become habitual, that is, they have carved out a psychological groove in their mind, and mere repentance is not enough to change this groove. It is necessary to carve out a new groove in its place and this is what one does by the process described above. The result is that instead of the faulty reaction, the new Christlike reaction takes place, often without even an effort. But it must be remembered that in all this process of reshaping our reaction we must rely on the inflowing of God's grace. In fact, sometimes through contemplation God will give us a virtue without any effort on our part, although usually he requires some effort as a token of our goodwill. But no amount of personal effort is sufficient of itself to acquire Christlike virtue.

To sum up then, it is contemplation that gives us light to see what virtue we should develop at any given time; it is contemplation that guides our efforts in trying to practise this virtue; and it is through contemplation that God eventually gives us the virtue. And as we become more perfect in the various virtues contemplation takes a deeper and stronger grip on our soul.

7

Doing God's Will: Making Decisions

Another way of looking at the practice of virtue is to think of it as doing God's will. Just as God has arranged the order of the universe, so too has he arranged the order of our lives. If we follow his arrangement we achieve the purpose for which we were created and experience a deep happiness and fulfilment notwithstanding the troubles which are everyone's lot in life. But if we deviate from his arrangement we bring disorder and misery into our lives which God never intended and we run the risk of losing him forever when this life is over. It is all-important, then, that we should know God's will for our life and live according to it.

In thinking about God's will people are often inclined to look to the future. They say,"I wish I knew what God wants me to do with my life". But they overlook the fact that God's will is here and now. Granted that we are living an honest life we can presume that our daily duties represent God's will for us. If we look at our daily life as it now is we can see that there are certain things that need to be done day by day. If we neglect to do them we feel a sense of guilt. These things are God's will for us.

It is not enough just to be doing the right things; we must do them for the right motive. People will do their daily duties simply because they have to be done, without any intention of pleasing God. That is not enough. And there are people who look upon some of life's duties as disagreeable chores to be got done with as quickly as possible so that they can get on to doing the things they really like. The word 'duty' has an unpleasant sound for many people. Yet duty is by no means always unpleasant. Our work is often interesting and enjoyable, and such things as eating, sleeping, rest and recreation are also duties and are God's will for us. But whatever might be God's will for us at any particular time, it is important that we should do it in order to please him. It is God who is giving us every moment of our lives and asking us to do something for him at each moment, as though he were saying to us, "Will you do this for me?" and we respond to him with an attitude which says, "Yes, Lord, it is for love of you".

An illustration will help to explain this attitude. Imagine a young couple who have just married and are deeply in love. They are about to go into their new house but a lot of work still needs to be done on it. It needs to be decorated and furnished and the garden has gone wild. Then suddenly the husband is called away on an important mission overseas in connection with his work. He will be away for about a year and circumstances make it impossible for his wife to accompany him. So she goes into the house alone and sets to work to put it in order. She works hard and her great desire is that when her husband returns he would be delighted to find such a lovely home awaiting him. This desire influences everything she does, giving her more energy than she thought she possessed, enabling her to overcome every difficulty and giving her a real sense of enjoyment in what would otherwise be a wearisome task. It is not that she is always actually thinking about her husband; more often her mind is occupied with her work, but her love for him is the power that influences everything she does.

So too it is that when we do God's will because we love him, this love becomes a power that influences our whole life. We give ourselves whole-heartedly and joyfully to our work, making light of difficulties, because we know God sees it all and we want him to be pleased. Our life becomes a sharing of love with God. His love gives us things to do and our love responds by the doing of them.

There will be many occasions, however, when the will of God is not obvious and we are faced with making a decision. It is then important that we should decide in accordance with God's will, and not according to our own selfish inclinations. This is particularly true of certain important decisions such as moving house, changing one's job, giving up a friendship, getting married, becoming a priest or a nun. The obvious thing a Christian will think of in these cases is to pray for guidance. But the mistake many people make is to expect a definite answer from God. They look for signs and attach great importance to coincidences. For example, they pray to a certain saint and then get a letter from a friend on the saint's feast-day suggesting an answer to their problem. They immediately take that as a sign from God that they should act on the suggestion contained in the letter. In fact, this might be quite a wrong decision. God can give signs when he wants to and when he does they will produce their effect in us automatically without our having to interpret them. But we must not be looking for signs because we can easily be mistaken in thinking that God has given us a sign, and even if he has, we can be mistaken in the way we interpret it.

How, then, are we to follow God's will in making a decision? Two things are necessary; we must use our mind in the ordinary way, and we must lean on God all the time while doing so. First of all we must investigate the facts of the situation, being careful to look at it from every angle. Then we must get a clear mental picture of the reasons in favour and balance it by a clear mental picture of the reasons against. In important matters it is helpful to get the opinions of other people whom we can trust. They will often help us to see things from quite a different angle. The final step is to weigh the two sides and pass judgment. This is the crucial act of decision. Reasoning has done its work. We must stop going back on reasons and see the situation as a whole and rely on our intuitive mind to form a decision.

So far I have described the psychological process. If a person goes through this process without God he will very likely make the wrong decision. If he goes through the process with God he will very likely make the right decision. To ask God's guidance in words is good but is not enough. What is needed is that deep underlying harmony of mind and will with God that comes with contemplation. Then God is working with us in all our thinking, in finding the facts, in weighing them up and in making our decision. And when we have made our decision we simply believe it is God's will. It is an act of faith but altogether unhesitating and certain. Because we have trusted God to guide us we believe that he has done so.

Of course our decision is not infallible. Apart from the assurance Christ gave his Church, infallibility does not exist on earth. It is possible that through human imperfection we might have made a mistake. But of one thing we can be absolutely certain: God will not allow the mistake to run too far; he will even turn it to greater good. This is because he values so much the trust we place in him. The Bible assures us frequently that anyone who trusts in the Lord will never be disappointed.

I have been speaking about decisions of considerable importance, but in smaller matters God-inspired decisions are made quite spontaneously by one who is in the habit of contemplating. This is due to a basic principle of contemplation, that when one is in harmony with the Source one is in harmony with everything that comes from the Source. The contemplative develops an instinct for God's will and is enlightened to see it in any given situation. In fact there are some matters in which God does not mind which way we decide as long as we have the intention of pleasing him, as, for example, whether we should go out for a walk or stay in and read.

8

How to Cope with Suffering

Once again I should like to call attention to the fact that I am speaking about developing harmony within ourselves so that God can flow into us freely in contemplation. Virtue puts our intellect and will in harmony with God. Doing God's will is the same harmony looked at in another way. But there is still a third way of viewing this same harmony. It consists in letting God do his will to us. According to circumstances sometimes one, sometimes another of these approaches will be the most obvious and practical. God is always doing things to us; he is always acting upon us through circumstances. Some things God wills directly; other things he does not will because they are sinful, but he permits them. But in all cases without exception it is his will that we react the right way to whatever happens to us. In this sense everything that happens to us is God's will and he wants us to accept it willingly as coming from him. Whether it is good or bad in itself he is using it to bring about good in our souls.

The things that happen to us can be divided into two main categories, pleasant and unpleasant. We accept pleasant things easily, but we do not always see the hand of God in them. In fact they often lead us to forget God, and that is why God often has to give us trouble, so that we will turn to him. God wants us to be happy but it is above all the everlasting happiness of heaven that he wants for us, and he loves us too much to give us earthly pleasures that would make us lose the everlasting pleasures of heaven. But when God sees that we react the right way to earthly pleasure he will give us a lot more of it although we can never get away from the condition of suffering that belongs to our fallen race.

What is the right reaction? It is to keep pleasure within suitable limits so that we do not neglect duty because of it: to think of God with love and gratitude as the giver of the pleasure, and to have a strong desire to show our appreciation of his goodness by serving him with greater fervour. I am speaking, of course, of pleasures that are good in themselves, because any pleasure that is sinful or leads to sin can never come from God.

There are also many experiences in life which are unpleasant and we can classify them under the general heading of suffering, and this can include everything from intense agony of mind or body to trivial inconveniences. The attitude of some people towards suffering is that it simply should not exist. Scientific progress, they believe, will eventually eliminate it and in the meantime it is best not to think about it and hope it will not happen to them. If suffering does come to such people they are thrown into despair and are apt to turn against God for allowing it to happen. The Christian attitude is that suffering is the result of sin but God has turned it into a means of salvation for those who are willing to accept it from his hand.

The all-important thing is acceptance, and this is an attitude that is widely misunderstood. The Church has been accused of telling people to be content with their lot instead of trying to improve their conditions. Let there be no doubt about it; God wants people to work in every possible way for a better world. It is sin that has thrown the world into disorder and we are struggling to remedy the effects of sin when we try to make the world a better place to live in. All praise to medical science and to many other sciences which have done so much to improve the conditions of human life. But in spite of all that has been done and is being done, suffering remains.

This is where acceptance comes in. Acceptance on the psychological level means facing up to our present state of suffering and learning to live with it even while we keep trying to cure it. Our mind should not be focussed on our suffering but on the living of our life. Psychiatrists attach great importance to acceptance. A patient cannot even begin a cure until he first of all learns to adapt to what actually is. Christian acceptance has something to add to the psychological attitude, namely the recognition of a divine purpose in suffering. God gives us suffering because he loves us; and if we accept it from him with gratitude and love it becomes a means of accomplishing great good.

What good does it accomplish? In the first place it has a healing influence on our soul. Sin has wounded our soul and even after it has been forgiven the wounds still remain and are gradually healed by suffering willingly accepted. Sin implies the seeking of some selfish pleasure and its wound is healed by the willing acceptance of God-given pain. Another way of looking at it is that there is a lump of evil in every one of us. It is the result of the sinful condition into which the human race has fallen. We cannot enjoy the happiness of intimacy with God until this lump has been broken down; and it is suffering willingly accepted that breaks it down. In other words God is like a surgeon performing an operation on a patient. He causes suffering in order to heal. He uses instruments, and these are the circumstances of life, oftentimes other people. A patient is not angry with the surgeon for hurting him and does not object to the use of instruments, because he sees the purpose of it all. So if we recognize God's loving purpose we can accept all he does for us.

Some kinds of suffering are easier to accept than others. Physical suffering is the easiest provided it is only that and no more. The reason is that our mind is free to turn to God. Mental-emotional suffering is more difficult because the mind gets swallowed up in the suffering and can scarcely detach itself in order to turn to God. I knew a woman who had an only child, a son to whom she clung with a possessive love that made his life a misery. He was in his twenties when he committed suicide, and the effect on his mother was shattering. She could not stop thinking about it and talking about it and she could not be consoled. Though she was a devout Catholic, her faith did not seem to help her; she could not detach her mind from her trouble and even felt it would be disloyal to her son to do so. When I last had contact with her she was heading for a nervous breakdown.

How is a person to accept that kind of suffering, to turn to God and see his loving purpose in it? The worst thing is to try to find intellectual answers as to why God should have allowed it. We cannot probe the mind of God and we must not expect to be able to understand his ways. We must simply believe that God knows what he is doing, that he is always right and always working for our good.

An ordinary discursive prayer-life is not enough to sustain a person through this kind of emotional turmoil. The feelings so take possession of the mind that prayer becomes almost impossible. But it is different with contemplation; and when I say contemplation I do not mean necessarily that a person has been setting aside time daily for silent, contemplative meditation. It is possible that while saying one's ordinary prayers devoutly, such as the Rosary or the Stations of the Cross, and turning to God during the day in heartfelt aspirations, a strong element of contemplation develops underneath and a person may not even realise it. But in a time of crisis it comes to the surface and takes over. Whatever way it comes, if the spirit of contemplation is present it saves a person at a time of deep emotional suffering. One is conscious of being firmly held by God and not allowed to sink under one's feelings. Although enveloped in turmoil one is looking above it and is at peace. Emotional suffering thus accepted by the power of contemplation is extremely valuable for the development of the soul.

A kind of suffering that involves special difficulty is the kind that comes to us from other people. Sometimes it might be of a serious nature but more often it consists of small daily irritations. The difficulty is that we focus our mind on the person who causes it and we forget to look towards God. People can hurt us in so many ways by what they say and how they behave, and we find ourselves having bitter thoughts against them. These thoughts go round and round in our mind disturbing and upsetting us. We get absorbed in our hurt feelings and in resentment towards the people who hurt us and we completely forget that God is at work. To prepare for these occasions we should have thought out our attitude well beforehand. God is a surgeon, he is performing an operation on us, these people are his instruments. We should thank God for what he is doing. We should keep our gaze fixed on God and not on the instruments he is using. Insofar as we do think of the people who are his instruments we should be thankful to them too for co-operating in God's purpose, even though they do not know it.

As a rule we should submit to the hurts that come to us from people without wanting to hit back. That is what Jesus taught us in the Sermon on the Mount. "If anyone strikes you on the right cheek, turn to him the other also." (Mt 5:38) But there may be times when we feel we have a duty to defend ourselves, as, for example, when false reports are spread about a person which endanger his job and his reputation, especially if he has a wife and children dependent on him. In such cases we may defend ourselves but we must be careful that we have a right motive in doing so. We must never act out of ill-will for another person or a desire for revenge. Two wrongs do not make a right. A right motive would be simply to safeguard our own interests, or to prevent the person who injured us from doing further evil to society, or perhaps even to bring about a reconciliation with him. But in all cases our attitude towards him personally should be one of goodwill, desiring what is best for him.

Finally, there are some things that people would not dignify by the name of suffering because they are so trivial, but yet they can come under this heading because they are things that happen to us rather than things we do. I refer to small daily disappointments and frustrations. We have an appointment and the person does not turn up. We want to take a walk and a visitor calls. We drop a plate and break it. The point is that our reaction in these cases is often the wrong one. We give way to a movement of impatience or annoyance, and we have lost an opportunity of accepting something for love of God. Our immediate reaction should be one of loving acceptance of what God has done to us. We do not get time to think; it has to be spontaneous, and only contemplation can give us this spontaneity.

Human suffering is a great problem for anyone who thinks about it. That is why so many people do not want to think about it. People ask why does God allow such terrible things to happen, even to little children who have done nothing to deserve it. If God is all-good and at the same time all-powerful, how can he allow these things?

A lot can be said by way of explanation, and even when all is said there is still no final answer. We have to make up our minds to it that in this world there is no final intellectual answer to the mystery of suffering. Christ himself did not give us an intellectual answer but he gave us a practical answer. He himself suffered and he invited us to follow him. It is interesting, though, that those people who have had near-death experiences and have come back to tell us about them, have said that they had an experience of universal knowledge, that they understood the meaning of the universe and that there was no question that did not have an answer. When they came back to normal life they no longer had that knowledge but they knew that they did have it.

There is no point then in torturing our minds by trying to understand how a loving God can allow so much suffering. What matters is that we recognize the divine purpose, and co-operate with it. I have already spoken of God's purpose in healing the wounds of our soul through suffering, but he also has another purpose: it is to unite us with the redemptive work of Christ.

Christ redeemed the whole world by his death and resurrection, that is, he saved us from the power of the evil spirit and opened up for us once more the way to God. But each one of us has to take hold of this redemption and make it his own. It is as though God were reaching out a hand to save us from drowning but we have to catch hold of it. This we do by believing in Christ and uniting our labours and sufferings with his, in fact allowing him to control our whole lives. We thus draw from the inexhaustible source of saving grace which Christ has merited by his death and resurrection in order to be freed from our sins and grow in the life of God. But we can win graces for other people as well. Merely by sharing in the sufferings of Christ we can share in his power of saving others. Of course Christ could do it all by himself but he wishes us to share in his work of redemption.

It is a great privilege but also a serious responsibility. A privilege because it makes us more Christlike and prepares us for a great reward in the kingdom of heaven; but a responsibility also because it means that some people are depending on us for their salvation. Therefore it is important to remember that when we bear our sufferings willingly in union with Christ, we are helping people in the best possible way, namely, by winning grace for them which helps them to overcome sin and live for God. We do not even know where those people are whom we are helping; it could be anywhere in the world. But we shall know when we meet them in heaven.

The Christian attitude towards suffering then can be summed up as follows: suffering is something to be remedied wherever possible because in general it is the result of sin, but at the same time it is to be accepted willingly because through the death of Christ it opens up for ourselves and others a way to share in his resurrected life.

9

How to Cope with our Emotions

Although our contact with God takes place essentially through our intellect and will, other parts of our personality have a considerable influence on this contact, particularly that area which can be described as our emotional nature. Our emotions or feelings (and I use these words with the same meaning) can be considered as halfway between body and spirit. It is the spirit or soul that gives them life but they show themselves through the body, as can easily be noticed when a person is angry, enthusiastic, depressed, etc. They can be divided into two main classes, disorderly and harmonious, or we might also call them negative and positive. Disorderly emotions can be very unpleasant and injurious. They eat up our vital energy to no purpose and leave us less capable of carrying on the duties of daily life. It is only too easy to see how feelings of anger, resentment, jealousy, bitterness of heart and many other negative feelings have an injurious effect. The vital question is how to deal with them.

It is generally recognized that repression is bad, that is, holding the emotion in and not allowing it to express itself in any way. In other words, keeping the lid on. If a negative emotion is repressed it develops interiorly and causes nervous disorders or even bodily illness. Therefore a person is advised to get it out of his system, to express it in some way. Imagine your enemy is beside you and shout your anger at him. Some would even say, confront him and have it out with him. It will clear the air and things will be better afterwards. But will they? More often you will have made things worse. And you will have deliberately indulged in a disorderly feeling which in itself is sinful. A better way is to relieve your feelings by talking to a friend about them, provided your friend will help you to calm these feelings and not make them worse.

But the really effective way of dissolving negative feelings is to change the underlying attitude from which they arise. Feelings arise from the attitudes that are deep in our hearts, that is, either from virtue or from the lack of virtue. If there is disorder in our hearts it will show by negative feelings, and the way to cure these feelings is by changing the inner attitude to one of virtue. When we develop the appropriate underlying virtue, then negative feelings are changed into positive ones. For example, when we have developed the virtue of meekness a thing that would formerly have made us angry no longer does so in a disturbing way, although we can be even more determined than ever to fight against injustice if need be. Or when we develop the virtue of patience we no longer feel resentment when misfortune comes to us, but rather a holy desire to share in the suffering of Christ.

Developing the appropriate virtue is the permanent way of dissolving negative feelings; but what are we to do in a sudden crisis? A virtue takes time to develop and so many things can happen to us before our virtues are strong enough to cope with them. The thing to do is: as soon as we are tempted by any disorderly feeling we must turn it immediately to God and allow his healing love to flow in upon it. We shall find that the disorder melts away immediately. We are saved for the moment but it is not a permanent cure. We have to keep turning the feeling to God as often as we are tempted by disorder, but in doing so we are gradually developing the virtue that we need and coming to a point when we shall not even be troubled by that disorderly feeling.

According as virtue develops in our hearts our emotions become harmonious or positive. Positive emotions are an important part of our personality and a valuable asset. We should not be afraid to let them be seen. And so many are indeed afraid. There are even some who think that showing emotion is a sign of immaturity and that the mature person is matter-of-fact and unemotional. The reason behind such thinking is that so many people do not have their emotions in order and they are afraid to let them be seen in case wrong emotions might come out. This is understandable and it is yet another reason in favour of the development of virtue, since virtue is the source of right emotion.

Just as beautiful clothes are an adornment of the body so right emotions are an adornment of the personality. We see this frequently in the saints, where the beauty of their souls shines out in their feelings. St Teresa of Avila was an outstanding example of this. She had an irresistible charm of manner which remained with her throughout her life. St John of the Cross had it also, although he was a quieter type of person and some people are inclined to regard him as a rather harsh ascetic. Yet when he was prior of a monastery in Spain and the community would have recreation after their midday meal, those who had been serving at table would leave their meal unfinished in order to get out quickly to listen to his conversation.

Not only is emotion an adornment of the personality, it is also a means of communication. Most of what we want to say can be expressed by words, but there are certain things that words cannot express. A glance of the eye, a touch of the hand can often say more than many words. Words can convey meaning but feelings can speak in depth, and as long as there is virtue in our hearts deep feelings will reveal inner beauty.

So far I have been speaking about feelings in general, now I should like to say something about them in connection with meditation. Feelings of devotion are frequently felt in discursive meditation, especially when one is in close communion with Jesus Christ in any of the scenes of his life. People are sometimes rather shy of these feelings and are inclined to suppress them because in some vague way they feel they are not right. But this is not correct. These feelings are good and they give intensity to our prayer, and even if they bring us deep enjoyment that is all right too provided we focus our attention, not on the enjoyment but on Christ. However, it would be wrong to start wanting these emotional feelings and to be dissatisfied when they do not come.

One reason why people are shy of their feelings in prayer is that they have often been told that "feelings do not matter". What this means is that if we are deprived of them and our prayer is dry and boring, it can still be very valuable if we persevere in it. The good will of our persevering effort is what matters to God, but if he gives us pleasant feelings we should accept them with simple gratitude. I knew a young Carmelite nun who before she entered the convent experienced great spiritual consolations from God in her contemplation, but when she entered the convent they all stopped and her soul was left in darkness and emptiness. She once complained to Our Lord about it, asking him why it was so, and he said to her: "You came here, not to enjoy my love but so that I could enjoy your love". That is something we should all remember when we seem to be getting nothing out of our meditation.

Instead, we can be giving a lot to God by our fidelity and perseverance.

It is in discursive meditation that our ordinary emotions have their place. In contemplation we go beyond not only thoughts and images, we go beyond our emotions as well. The normal attitude, at least in the early stages of contemplation, is one of calm, peaceful attentiveness. Sometimes we have to make a certain effort to hold ourselves in that state because the attraction of God is not yet strong enough. At other times God holds us so that we do not notice the passing of time and we even think we have fallen asleep. Although we feel deeply happy there is no emotion, or if occasionally some emotion might well up, we reject it immediately because we feel it would spoil the purity of the contemplation.

While this is true of ordinary emotions, God can produce spiritual feelings in us when he wishes. These are quite different. They are not the result of any effort on our part. They are produced by God, and at a much deeper level than our ordinary emotions. Sometimes it is a feeling of love, which we experience as a warmth in the region of the heart; sometimes it is painful as well, as though it were a burning fire, and yet it is accompanied by an exquisite sweetness and a deep sense of the presence of God.

God might also produce in us feelings of compunction, a piercing sorrow for our sins and for the sins of the world, together with an ardent desire to make atonement to God by greater love, and at the same time we experience peace, joy and gratitude that Christ has triumphed over sin by his death and resurrection. All these feelings are summed up in what is known as the gift of tears. This is far different from ordinary tears of devotion. It is something produced in us by God, altogether beyond our own efforts. It has a profound effect on our souls, cleansing away the stains of sin and filling us with love for God. This is not the kind of experience that should be ignored in contemplation. Rather it should be desired and prayed for.

It is clear, then, that our emotional nature has an important part to play both in our relationship with God and in our relationship with people. But it is equally important that it be brought under the control of the spirit. Our feelings have been thrown into a state of disorder by sin and they easily react to situations in a way that is unreasonable and that brings a lot of unnecessary suffering into our lives. But if gradually with the help of contemplation we bring them under the control of God, we come to experience a new delight in living and we can prepare our souls to receive those deeper feelings that come from God.

10

How to Cope with the Sex Instinct

I have just explained how disorderly emotions can be dissolved by changing the underlying attitude of heart from which they spring into a virtuous attitude. But it is different with an instinct. An instinct cannot be dissolved. It is a vital power, and the problem is to direct this power into a suitable channel.

I am thinking now particularly of the sex instinct because it has such a strong influence on human behaviour. As in the case of negative feelings, repression here, too, is bad. It can lead to withdrawal from people, especially from the opposite sex, to a turning in upon oneself and to various neurotic disorders. On the other hand, to give unrestrained expression to the instinct is not the answer either, although this advice is sometimes given, even by psychiatrists. We have only to look at the daily papers to see the evils caused by unrestrained sex: broken homes and broken hearts, violence and even murder. But what about solitary sex indulgence, where no one is injured? Looking at this now only from the point of view of its relationship to contemplation, it is the very opposite and contradiction of all that contemplation stands for. Contemplation is a going out from self, from thoughts, images, emotions, and a handing over of ourselves to God, whereas solitary sex-indulgence is a turning in upon oneself. It is selfishness, but a special kind of selfishness; selfishness at a deep level. It cuts deeply into a person's being. We are all ashamed of being thought selfish even in the smallest thing. How careful we are at meals to be thoughtful for others and not to appear anxious to get what we want for ourselves. If selfishness is so repulsive, even in small things, how evil must it be when it penetrates deeply into our nature through disordered sex.

If repression is bad and unrestrained outlet is bad, then how is this instinct to be dealt with? The obvious answer one might give is self-control, yet to many this would seem to be just another way of saying repression. The real answer is by what we call sublimation. Sublimation means denying the instinct its immediate outlet and directing its vital energy to a higher purpose. A very simple illustration will explain this. Imagine a four-storey house in which the water supply has to be pumped to the upper stories. It can happen that if it is being tapped off at the intermediate stories, little or none gets to the top, but if the taps on the lower floors are closed, the full force of the water goes to the top.

Partial sublimation has its place in marriage, because consideration for one's partner will often be a reason for restraint. Another reason would be the practice of the rhythm method of birth-control. But this restraint is not repression because the vital energy of the instinct is directed towards a higher purpose. This higher purpose is spiritual friendship, and ideally speaking it should lead in to a friendship with God. Spiritual friendship is the bond that holds a marriage together and gives real happiness and fulfilment to the partners. Sexual intercourse will not achieve this, and people who think they need to have intercourse before marriage in order to get to know each other are mistaken. What they need to cultivate before marriage is spiritual friendship. But granted that in marriage this relationship exists, then sexual intercourse has something positive to add. It puts a stamp on the friendship, sets a seal on it. It is as though it puts the friendship in a definite framework and gives it a definite shape and form.

Complete sublimation is required in celibacy. This involves a complete denial of physical sex, and the vital energy of the instinct in this case is entirely directed towards a higher purpose, but in this case the higher purpose is not friendship with another human person but friendship with God. This requires a greater effort of restraint and considerable struggle because the instinct is being denied all its immediate outlet, but the vital energy is not repressed because it is being pushed up to its highest outlet, namely, to the development of friendship with God.

According as this friendship with God becomes rooted in the soul of the celibate, he becomes free to develop friendship with people, whether of the same or of the opposite sex, and such friendship is free from self-seeking. The deeper his union with God the more he is capable of intimacy with people. Consecrated celibacy can be a genuine state even when intimacy with God is not well developed but in this case it is accompanied by a certain insecurity and danger of giving way to the instinct.

People who are celibate, not as a result of consecration to God, but merely by force of circumstances, are psychologically in the same position as the consecrated celibate. Only intimacy with God can give them security and an ability to form genuine friendships. People who are keeping company with a view to marriage are committed to temporary celibacy, but with a difference. In their case the vital energy of the sex instinct is directed towards forming a spiritual friendship with each other, a friendship which ideally should be a means of helping them to get closer to God.

In all cases spiritual friendship is the goal towards which the vital energy of the sex instinct is directed, whether the direct aim is friendship with God, as in permanent celibacy, or human friendship as in marriage or leading up to marriage. It is obvious, of course, that even in marriage or company-keeping the individuals will seek God, each in their own way in the living of their Christian lives, but what I want to emphasize is that their mutual friendship should itself be a means of leading them closer to God.

I have frequently mentioned spiritual friendship; now I want to give a few headings to indicate what it consists in. The first is a common purpose. The second is a sharing of ideas and feelings. The third is a centering on God.

It is difficult if not impossible to establish a friendship unless two people have something to do together. It might be just playing golf together or sharing the same hobbies. When two people meet casually at a social and are attracted to each other they immediately start trying to discover what they have in common. If people have nothing worthwhile in common they tend to seek their fulfilment directly in each other and this results in disillusionment and frustration. It is called the 'face-to-face' attitude and is like finding oneself in a cul-de-sac instead of on a through road. The correct attitude is 'side-by-side' working towards a common purpose. Married life supplies an ideal framework for this 'side-by-side' relationship because the partners are committed to a life-long work in common, developing their home and educating their children. If they genuinely work together for the same purpose they are drawn closer to each other all the time. As any two objects move towards the same centre, they get closer to each other as they approach their common aim.

In order that this intimacy can develop the second condition is necessary, namely, that there be a sharing of ideas and feelings. Otherwise there would be no deep cooperation. The aim of such sharing is to achieve unity. So they listen to each other, try to understand each other, and are willing to give in to each other for the sake of unity. In this way their personalities are opened up to each other and the inner core of each one's being is revealed to the other. This is personal contact at a deep level of the spirit and it brings with it intense happiness to both. But it must be remembered that this only happens when there is mutual self-sacrifice for a common purpose.

As this spiritual friendship is in itself a natural human condition it can exist even when there is no faith in God, if people are naturally tolerant and even-tempered. But in this case it could not be called supernatural and would have no value for eternal life. As St Paul says, without faith it is impossible to please God. In fact, considering how self-centred we are, it will usually be impossible to develop such a friendship without continual help from God. Hence the third condition is required, namely, that the people concerned should centre their efforts on God, and draw from him the enlightenment and the strength they need. This is where contemplation becomes the great unifying power in their lives. Their common work is a focus for unity but it is not the final focus. Beyond it there is God, towards whom everything should be directed and from whom comes a power that draws all things to himself. They surrender to this power in contemplation, and as God draws them deeper into his being he draws them to each other in an intimacy that can be described as mystical. A special word needs to be said about spiritual friendship developed directly towards God, as in the case of permanent celibacy. Here, too, the three conditions are the same but they are applied differently.

First, a common purpose. The celibate works in partnership with Christ to do whatever work has been assigned to him by God's will. Second, a sharing of ideas and feelings. The celibate studies the teachings of Christ and brings his own ideas into accordance with them. He opens his heart to Christ in prayer, allowing the light of contemplation to fill him with the Spirit of Christ. Third, a centering on God. Through Christ, with Christ and in Christ he is drawn deeply into the godhead. It is true that married people, as individuals, should aim immediately at this friendship with God also, but the point I want to make clear is that the vital energy of the sex instinct, which in married people is to some extent diverted towards human friendship, is for the celibate totally directed towards friendship with Christ. Human friendships, for the celibate, will result from his friendship with Christ, rather than lead towards it.

11

The Cross of Christ

One usually thinks of the principle of sublimation in connection with the sex instinct but in fact it can apply to all our instincts. All our vital powers or faculties have an instinct or natural urge for their proper objects, such as an eye for seeing, the ear for hearing, the tongue for speaking, the mind for thinking, the will for loving. Had human nature not been damaged by sin, these instincts would have worked in harmony with each other and for the general good of the person as a whole, but when man rebelled against God by sin the other faculties rebelled against man himself, each now wanting to go its own way regardless of the real good of the person who owns them. It is like the difference between an army commanded by a capable general who co-ordinates the activities of the various units into a unified striking-force against the enemy, and on the other hand an army where the general and his staff have been killed and there is no longer any central control, so that each unit is on its own, doing what it likes, and thus the army disintegrates.

Our faculties desire to follow their own inclinations regardless as to whether it is good for us or not. We do indeed have power to control them and direct their activities towards our personal welfare, but this can be a difficult task and only too easily do we give in to the pleasure they afford us even when it is against our true interests. Thus to give in to them dissipates their vital energy in a way that is unproductive and lessens our ability to work towards our genuine welfare. An obvious example is that of a person who does not control his drinking habits so that his work suffers and the peace of his home is disturbed. Or a person who enjoys the company of his friends so much that he has no time left for meditation.

To apply here the principle of sublimation means to deny our faculties their immediate satisfaction so that their vital energy may be directed towards a higher good. By a higher good is meant whatever activity God wishes us to be engaged in at any given time, and ultimately the desire for God himself. Does this mean that we should deny ourselves all pleasure? No; but it means that we should never seek pleasure directly for its own sake. Pleasure should be regarded as a by-product, something in the nature of a condiment. Salt can give flavour to a meal, but no one would dream of making a meal of salt itself. Therefore it is right to do pleasurable things and enjoy the pleasure of them, provided the thing itself is God's will and we are doing it because God wants us to do it.

In order, then, to sublimate the energy of our faculties, three things are required:

(1) To have the intention of doing what God wants us to do at this particular moment. Our conscience will tell us what we ought to be doing and show us how to keep our priorities right.

(2) We should try to do well whatever we do, giving ourselves whole-heartedly, but in a calm, relaxed manner and without anxiety. It does not matter if we are unable to do it as well as we would wish. It is our effort and good-will that are important. We should take a pride in our work, doing it, in a sense, for its own sake and not merely for any ulterior motive such as making money, although that of course can be a consideration also. The same applies to our amusements. We enjoy them thoroughly but we keep them in their proper place and do not allow them to interfere with other things. The fact is that any work or other occupation God gives us to do has an intrinsic value that nourishes our spirit, provided we give ourselves generously to the doing of it. In other words, if we give ourselves to our work with a good spirit it will normally give us considerable enjoyment. God has arranged it so because he wishes us to enjoy doing his will, and our enjoyment is none the less because we are not focussing our attention on it but rather on the doing of God's work. Apart from the pleasure of doing our work well there is also the additional and greater pleasure of doing it as a loving response to God. It is as though at every moment God were saying to us, "Will you do this for me?" and we were saying, "Yes, Lord, I am doing it for you".

(3) In order to be able to do our work well for God and to enjoy the pleasure that goes with it, we need to be on the alert to deny ourselves any selfish inclination to seek our own pleasure directly.

This is where we deny our faculties their immediate outlet in order to sublimate their energies into the doing of God's work and enjoying it for his sake. Selfishness is always likely to enter into even the noblest of our activities. We can waste our time in various ways with no other purpose than that we feel like doing it. To deny these selfish inclinations is a self-denial that leads to enjoyment and fulfilment. And what might come as a surprise to many people, it is also a sharing in the cross of Christ. Just as the cross consists of two beams, one of which cuts right across the other, so we cut right across the line of our selfishness by directing our energy to the doing of God's will, and this sacrificial attitude brings us peace and joy.

However, it can frequently happen that doing or accepting God's will can bring us real pain, whether this be pain of body or perhaps more frequently pain of heart, which we usually call hurt feelings. It is here that sublimation is more especially needed in order to transform ordinary suffering into the cross of Christ. Just as our faculties instinctively seek their pleasure, so also they instinctively seek to escape from pain. This is their selfish reaction which takes no account of the good of the person as a whole, and just as their energy is dissipated by pleasure so also it is dissipated by their avoidance of pain. Sublimation here consists in denying the pain-escaping tendency in order to direct the vital energy of the faculties towards the doing or accepting of God's will.

In order to accomplish this three things are required:

(1) Take what practical steps are possible to relieve the pain or remove its causes. If you are ill, seek medical aid. If you are unhappy where you live or work, seek better conditions. If you have a quarrel with a friend, try to bring about reconciliation. And so on with other things.

(2) While trying to remedy a painful situation give it only the minimum amount of thought that is necessary. Apart from this, refuse to think about the situation and its causes. To continue such thinking would mean allowing your faculties to indulge in their selfish, pain-escaping tendencies without any purpose, and would drain away their vital energies.

(3) While not thinking about the situation that is causing the pain, look straight into the pain itself. Let the pain go right into you. Welcome it, desire it and go through it to God. When we welcome pain we let go our clinging to pleasure and God is able to lift us up to himself. Think of a child sitting on the ground while the father wants to take him up in his arms. But the child is clinging on to an iron bar on the ground and will not let go, so his father cannot lift him up until the child lets go his hold on the bar.

So, too, we must let go our selfish clinging before God can lift us up, and this we do when we welcome pain.

In pain thus welcomed we meet Christ. He is waiting for us in the pain. The pain opens up for us a pathway to Christ and along this pathway he draws us into the mystery of his cross. Our pain is transformed through the power of his cross. It is no longer ordinary suffering. A divine power has entered into it and a divine love. Through our union with his cross the power of Christ's resurrection is already at work in us. We are being lifted above our selfishness and we are experiencing a spiritual joy even in our pain, the joy of knowing that in our own small way we are sharing in the work Christ came to do, and that through his suffering and death we shall share in the ultimate joy of his resurrection.

We think of Christ giving us his cross when some great suffering comes to us, such as a serious illness or the death of a dearly loved friend, but to associate the cross only with sufferings of this kind makes us feel we do not want to get too close to Christ lest he might give us too many crosses.

This is a mistaken attitude. In nearly everybody's life there are from time to time great sufferings, but mostly the troubles of life consist of small daily irritations and upsets. When we turn to Christ he simply takes our life as it is and gives new meaning to our troubles by drawing them up into the transforming power of his cross. Our suffering is far less when we are united with Christ. We are freed from the suffering caused by our own selfishness, by anger, resentment, self-pity, bitterness or despair. And whatever pain we do have to bear is shot through by the joy-giving power of his resurrection which is always at work in those who carry his cross.

Where we lose out, however, is that we do not recognize the cross in small things. Jesus tells us to take up our cross daily, and it is true to say that scarcely a day passes that there are not many minor frustrations and irritations to put up with, but because we do not realize that Christ is presenting us with his cross we give way to our selfish feelings on these occasions.

A man is doing a job in his office and someone has taken away a reference book that he needs. He becomes angry and complains about how careless and inconsiderate people are. He does not realize that Christ is offering him the cross. He should relax and open up to the pain of this frustration, letting it go right into him as something good. He should not allow his mind to brood on the cause of his inconvenience, but at the same time he should make gentle and polite enquiries as to who has taken his reference book.

A housewife is cooking a meal and her children start quarrelling. She goes to quiten them down and meanwhile something gets burnt on the stove. What Christ is asking her to do is to relax and willingly bear the pain of this upset.

Driving a car provides many opportunities for bearing the cross. Other drivers will sometimes do reckless, discourteous things. The irritation this causes us is a pain that Christ asks us to bear, he wants us to suffer our feelings without brooding on them.

If we think over the various circumstances of our daily lives we shall find many occasions where we suffer pain in our feelings. It can happen at business meetings, in playing games, at parties, or even in casual conversations with our friends. But we must be alert to see the cross of Christ in everything that irritates our feelings no matter how small the occasion might be. To do this will bring great happiness into our lives, and we shall be surprised at the ease with which we shall be able to cope with more serious troubles whenever they arise.

12

Humility

A virtue of particular importance for the development of contemplation is the virtue of humility. The word "humility" comes from the Latin "humus" meaning "the ground". The virtue itself means having a lowly opinion of ourselves, which results from recognizing our true relationship towards God, which is one of utter dependence. But it does not at all mean that we are supposed to think that we are no good. Some people do think they are no good, that they can never succeed at anything, that they do not deserve to succeed, and if they find they are being successful at something they even feel compelled to make it go wrong. That is not humility, it is a psychological defect possibly due to the way they were treated as children.

God has made us in his own image, and so in a small way everyone reflects the beauty of God. And God has given us gifts of many kinds, physical, mental, spiritual. We should recognize these gifts in ourselves, not to be proud of them as though they were our own, but in order to give God the credit for having given them to us, and in order to have a proper sense of responsibility as to how we use them. If something is our own property we can do what we like with it, use it, give it away, destroy it. We have full rights over it. But if in business we are given money for a particular purpose we must use it for that purpose and render an account of how we used it. This is how we must regard the gifts God has given us. He gives them to us so that we should use them the way he wants them used, and he wants us to render an account to him as to how we have used them, and we shall be rewarded or punished according as we have used them well or badly. This is what Jesus teaches us in the parable of the talents. (Mt 25:14-30)

We must take care, then, that we use our gifts according to God's will. Sometimes he gives us gifts that he does not want us to use but rather to sacrifice for his sake. I knew a girl who was strongly attracted to nursing, but she also had a musical gift that would have made her an outstanding concert pianist. She realized that she could not develop both of these at the same time and she prayed for God's guidance. And God told her that if she wanted to save her soul she must not be a concert pianist. She listened to him and became a nurse.

While admitting the excellence of our being and the gifts we have received from God, we recognize that nothing we have is our own and that we must depend on God's continual help for the right use of our gifts, in fact for our every thought and action, since we can do nothing without God. It is true that once God has given us our being he will never take it from us, but as to how we live, we shall continually be making mistakes, committing sins and bringing trouble on ourselves unless we constantly lean upon God for guidance and support. Thus to keep turning to God for help at all times is true humility. We easily recoil against doing this because we feel it limits our freedom and independence. There can be many good reasons for being independent of other people but there is no good reason for wanting to be independent of God. The truth is that we are dependent on him and the only sensible thing is to live according to this truth.

This spirit of independence, which is so much against humility, is often seen in our intellectual activity. We feel we are sincerely searching for religious truth and spiritual development, but we want to work it out for ourselves and we do not want God to tell us. That is pride, and instead of finding the truth we shall get lost in the complexity of our own ideas. God wants us to humble ourselves before him in love, asking him to lead us ever more deeply into the truth and receiving it from his hand as a little child would from his teacher. We are all children before God and in his presence we must forget our mature, independent ways.

Taking our stand on our own inherent nothingness, we recognize God in all his creation. We recognize him in the beauties of nature and in the wonders of the universe and we have a sense of wonder and admiration when we think about these things. We feel we owe it to God to do what we can to preserve the beauty of his world, to remedy anything that would disfigure the landscape or contaminate the environment. We also recognize God's work in other people and the gifts he has given them. There is an inherent goodness in every one although it may be disfigured by many human imperfections. We overlook the human imperfections, which are not the work of God, and treat people with respect because of the gifts God has given them.

Every human person is valuable in God's sight and is made in God's image, although this image is in the soul where we cannot see it except by faith. But it means that in a sense we should worship God in every person we meet by treating them with respect and even with a certain reverence. It is as though we in our nothingness bow down before the gifts of God in them. This too is humility, and it explains what the saints have meant when they said that we should regard ourselves as the least of all.

Our respect is not only for people but even for the things around us, furniture in our room, the utensils in the kitchen, even the clothes we wear. All these are God's gifts to us and we show our gratitude to God by the respect and care with which we use them. We must be quite clear in our minds that all things come from God no matter how many human agencies are at work in providing us with them. We know what it is to possess something which has a sentimental value for us, how we treasure it, not for its own sake for it might be a thing of no value such as a picture postcard, but because it was given to us by a dearly-loved friend. So too everything we have is a gift from the God who loves us more than anyone else, and for this reason it should have for us what we might call a sentimental value. It speaks to us of the love of him who gave it and asks of us a response of loving gratitude. We can get into the habit of consciously thanking God for things, but through contemplation we develop an attitude of deep and constant thanksgiving which expresses itself by the care with which we use things and keep them clean and tidy.

Thus, taking our stand on our own nothingness we express our worship to God by an attitude of respect and reverence with regard to everything he has done whether for ourselves or for others. We humble ourselves before the whole of creation for love of the Creator.

But this humility is not easily come by because there is a hard core of pride in every one of us. We want our independence, not realizing that only by submission to God can we be really free and happy. Before sin entered the world human nature was God-centred. Sin broke that harmony, turning us back in on ourselves, making us self-centred and wanting an independence that we cannot have. This is what pride is. In many people it is not obvious and on the surface they seem humble enough, but deep within them is this hard core of unwillingness to yield up the ownership of their being to God.

How, then, is this pride to be broken down? The obvious answer is, by cultivating the virtue of humility, but there is a peculiar difficulty about cultivating this virtue, because the roots of pride go so deeply into the spirit. We must ponder on the meaning of humility, desire it and ask God for it. If there is one word more than another that will guide us in our search for humility, it is the word "submission". This implies not just an external compliance but an inner willingness of our heart to submit. We submit to the doing of God's will, and we submit to letting God do what he likes to us, as I have already explained. The more willingly we submit to everything that happens to us, not complaining or criticizing but praising and thanking God regardless of our feelings, the more surely God will break down our pride, thus removing what is perhaps the greatest obstacle of all to our intimacy with him.

People sometimes think that humility makes a person weak and spineless but in fact it does just the opposite. It is pride that makes a person weak. A proud person is afraid of what people will think of him. He is afraid to undertake certain works in case he might fail and people would laugh at him. He is very sensitive about "losing face". But the humble person, by submitting to God and so being sure of his guidance, is quite fearless. As long as he knows he is pleasing God he does not care whether he succeeds or fails. And he does not care who is against him because he knows that God is with him.

13

Conscience

God made a world of harmony and appointed laws to govern everything in creation so that the entire work of his hands should manifest a splendid unity and beauty. Lower forms of nature operate automatically according to God's plan but we humans are expected to submit ourselves freely to his laws. But because we are free we have the power also of going against them. But when we do we feel a certain conflict within ourselves, our disordered will working against the basic tendency of our being towards God. This is what we call our conscience.

If a person is deeply embedded in selfishness he will scarcely notice this disorder; his conscience is dull. But as a person grows in spiritual enlightenment his conscience becomes very sensitive and he would be aware of the least movement against God's will. If everyone were highly developed spiritually and intimately united with God, then conscience alone would be a sufficient guide for human life, because a person would quickly be able to discern God's will in every circumstance. But our minds are so clouded by ignorance and we are so little attuned to spiritual realities and evil often has such an attraction for us, that in a great many cases our conscience would be unable to discern the will of God. For this reason God has made it easier for us to get to know his laws by telling them to us in plain language through men specially chosen for the purpose.

Thus he gave us the ten commandments through Moses. Our own thinking should have made them known to us in any case, but God wanted to make them absolutely clear, so he told us. Then there is the law which Christ gave us and which adds a new dimension to the harmony of the universe. It is the law of the children of God, redeemed by Christ and can be seen especially in the Sermon on the Mount. (Matthew chapters 5, 6 and 7.) For example: Blessed are those who suffer persecution; love your enemies; do not be anxious about your life. Christ told his Church to make his teaching known to the whole world, and the Church has no power to change anything that has come from Christ. But the Church has power to make its own laws, and the purpose of these is to apply the unchanging law of Christ in a manner suited for different times and cultures.

Because God has given us these clearly-defined laws it is now much easier for conscience to register harmony or disharmony with them than if a person had to rely entirely on his own spiritual enlightenment, which in so many cases is very defective. It is important to remember that the whole value of conscience consists in its relationship with the harmony of God's universe. Therefore it is necessary for us to get to know the laws by which God governs his universe, at least those which pertain to human life. In other words we must educate our conscience to a knowledge of God's law and the law of Christ as communicated to us by the Church. If we fail to do this, conscience comes to mean for us simply our own opinion. A thing becomes right or wrong for us simply because we think so. This is not conscience at all. Conscience applies God's law to our lives, but we are wanting to be a law for ourselves.

When conscience registers disharmony and a person goes ahead in spite of it and does what he wants, he experiences what we call the pangs of conscience. This is the painful feeling of conflict between his disordered will and the order established by God. If he continues acting against his conscience these pangs gradually get less and he develops hardness of heart. This does not happen quickly, and in the meantime it is a painful state to be in because he knows he is guilty. So what a person usually tries to do is to find reasons to convince himself that he is not doing wrong, and this to some extent takes away the sense of guilt. This is called rationalization. It makes a person feel more at peace in his wrongdoing but it is an even greater disorder than before because now both the mind and the will are out of harmony with God, whereas previously, although the will was wrong, the mind admitted its guilt. In fact this rationalization can go so far that a person will tell you that he is sincerely convinced that what he is doing is right. But he is not sincere. He lost his sincerity when he began to rationalize.

What should you do when conscience registers disharmony?

Simply admit your guilt. Many people think that guilt-feelings are bad. They are not; they are the expression of a true state of things. You should react by repentance, and if you feel you cannot repent you should ask God to help you to do so. Once you repent, God forgives the sin; and that is the end of the guilt.

Sometimes guilt feelings persist, even for years. This is a different kind of guilt. It is not moral guilt, which is removed when we repent and are forgiven. It is psychological guilt which means that we refuse to forgive ourselves. This is due to pride and an unwillingness to accept a tarnished image of ourselves. The remedy lies in humility. It is true that after moral guilt is removed there is still atonement to be made. Damage can be caused in an instant but repairing it takes time. Boys playing ball in the street break a shop window. They apologize to the shopkeeper, who says "All right, it was an accident, I forgive you. But it will take time to have it repaired and I shall have to send the bill to your father". When a sin is committed the harmony of God's universe has in some way been injured, and the sinner has to repair this over some space of time, not by torturing himself with a sense of guilt which would achieve nothing, but by a more whole-hearted loving service of God.

The valuable thing about conscience is not just that it makes us know that we have sinned but it warns us when we are in danger of sinning. Sin does not take place until we deliberately give in to a disorderly inclination, but conscience has already begun to make us feel this disorder so that we have time to consider whether we are going to resist it or give in. Passion often blinds our mind so that we give in easily and feel sorry for it afterwards. We excuse ourselves by saying we did not really mean to do wrong, but the real sin lay in the fact that we had not developed a habit of prayer.

Prayer, particularly contemplative prayer, makes us very alert in reacting against any disharmony towards God. This is why contemplative meditation is not just a luxury; it can sometimes be the only thing that will enable us to resist a sudden strong temptation. Contemplation brings us into direct contact with God, who is the Source of all Being, of all the laws of the universe, and as we thus develop harmony with the source we develop harmony with everything that comes from it. So as contemplation gets stronger we instinctively and strongly react against any disharmony that conscience registers.

14

Compunction of Heart

It is comparatively easy to see sin as disorder, as being an injury to the harmony of God's universe, although perhaps more frequently we judge sin on a human level with little or no reference to God. We think of it as something repugnant to our human sense of values. Thus certain things we unhesitatingly regard as evil, such as murder or adultery, but other things that are regarded as sins do not seem very wrong to us, as when a Roman Catholic without any excuse neglects Sunday Mass. This is because we think of sin on a natural, human level. But something has happened that puts sin into an entirely different dimension. It is the fact that God has called us to share his own life. In other words, we are called to a supernatural life. If God had left us on the level of human life, then we would be right in seeing sin as disorder and nothing more, and the reward of a well-lived human life would be a human happiness, that is, living in a world free from all evil and suffering where people would be united in universal love and where, through a highly-developed contemplative power, they would enjoy God as the Source of Being, shining through his creation. But they would not see God as he is in himself. They would not even know that there was such a thing as the blessed Trinity.

But God decided not to leave us on the merely human level but to open up to us the inner life of his godhead. For this purpose he reveals himself personally to every individual, offering them in one way or another the gift of faith. There is no option to choose either natural or supernatural happiness. God's invitation to share his own life is such a privilege that to refuse it would be an insult to God. When we accept it an intensely personal element is introduced into our relationship with him. Had we remained on the natural level our contact with God would have been a blissful experience indeed but yet impersonal. We would only be contacting him as the Source of Being, shining through his creation. But now that he has invited us to share in the life of his holy Trinity a wonderful personal relationship has begun. We are drawn into that mysterious process by which God the Father is eternally begetting his Son, and Father and Son eternally breathing out their love in the Holy Spirit. Provided our lives are directed towards God, this divine life continues to develop in us here on earth. We cannot see it although we are aware of the effects it produces in our soul. After death we enter into the full enjoyment of it. We shall share in God's own happiness. We shall know in a small way what it feels like to be God.

A person might say: what difference does it make whether we contact God in a natural way or a supernatural way, is it not the same God anyway? It is indeed the same God, but the manner of contacting him is very different. An illustration will help to explain this. Suppose you are working in a large factory. The owner of the factory comes around from time to time to meet his workers and have a few pleasant words with them. You are justified in saying you know him. But suppose for some reason he takes a liking to you and says, "Come to my office and have a chat". You both discover that you have many things in common, and soon you are invited to your boss's home to meet his wife and family. As time goes on you become a frequent visitor at his home and become very much one of the family. You even go on holidays with them. It is the same man with whom you are now on terms of intimate friendship whom you once knew merely as owner of the factory. But what a difference there is in the relationship! This helps us to understand the difference between knowing God in a natural way as showing himself through creation, and knowing him in a supernatural way as sharing his divine life.

This fact of being called to share in God's life puts sin into an entirely different dimension. Sin is still a disorder but now it is very much more. It is a personal insult. Going back to the illustration, suppose you used your privileged position with your boss to steal from him large sums of money while all the time pretending to be his trusted friend. That, surely, would be base ingratitude and insult, far worse than if the same money were stolen by another worker in the factory.

There is a further element in sin which is the most mysterious of all and quite baffles our understanding. There is something infinite about the evil of sin. The goodness of God is infinite, that is, it has no limits or boundaries of any kind. Therefore there is something infinitely evil about offending God, who is infinitely good. That is why the human race was incapable of saving itself from sin. It had nothing infinite to offer God to make atonement for sin. It was God himself who solved the problem for us. He gave us someone who is God and man at the same time, Jesus Christ. As man he was able to act on our behalf; as God he was able to offer infinite atonement for sin. Now we can atone for our sins when we unite our loving repentance with his great act of atonement, his death on the cross. Although this concept of sin baffles our minds, it does bring home to us the unimaginable evil that is contained in any sin.

It would be wrong to react to this fact by anxiety and worry as to how much we have sinned. This would only disturb our soul and do us no good. But we should admit that we are sinners — we all are — and turn to Christ with deep sorrow for our sins that through him we may be healed and sanctified.

This is what is meant by compunction of heart. It suggests a piercing sorrow for sin that touches the depths of our being, a sorrow that we have offended someone who loves us so much, yet joy and gratitude that we have been saved through the death of Christ, and a great upsurge of love impelling us to plunge deeply into that divine heart which loves us so much. This compunction of heart is something we should greatly desire, not by torturing ourselves with self-centred reproaches about our sins, but by seeing them as a betrayal of love and wanting to make up to God by loving him more and more.

Nothing opens our souls so much to the inflowing of contemplation as this hatred of sin inspired by love of God, and indeed it is contemplation itself that gives us this compunction of heart and brings it to perfection. Granted that we have the desire for it, God will do the rest through contemplation.

15

Freedom

One of the effects of contemplation is that it leads the soul into freedom. Freedom is one of our deepest desires. This is because God has given us a free will, and we rebel against anything that would limit its freedom, and unfortunately we never seem to possess fully the freedom we desire.

Freedom can be described as the joyous and spontaneous self-expression of a perfect nature. We feel we are really free only when we can do exactly whatever we like; yet if ever we try to do this we very quickly run into trouble. The reason is that our nature is not perfect; it has been seriously wounded and thrown into disorder by sin. There is both good and bad in us, and if we express ourselves freely both good and bad come out and the bad enslaves the good. Suppose a young man has a great desire to be a top-ranking athlete. Freedom for him means the attainment of this goal. He understands the intensive training he must undergo in order to achieve this, but he wants to be free to do other things as well. He wants to eat big meals and stay up late nearly every night drinking with his friends. He thinks to himself, "I do not want to be tied down. I value my freedom. I want to do as I please." What happens? His life of self-indulgence makes him utterly unfit to achieve what he really wants more than anything else, namely, to be an outstanding athlete. The bad came up as well as the good and spoiled the good; using "bad" here in the sense of things injurious to his purpose.

Or take another example. A student wants to pass an examination in order to qualify for a career that he has set his heart on.

More than anything else he wants to be free to have this career. But he wants to be free for other things as well, to go out with his friends, go to shows, play games and he spends so much time doing these things that he fails his examination and loses his career. Wanting to be free for everything, he lost his freedom in the most important thing.

When God first made man he gave him a perfect nature so that he could do all he wanted to do and it would be right. But sin threw human nature into a state of disorder and slavery with the result that now we have to struggle hard in order to carve out for ourselves an area of freedom. The athlete has to submit to rigorous training, denying himself many pleasures, in order to get what he wants. Likewise the student has to submit to the discipline of study in order to get what he wants. In a word, freedom is possible only at the cost of discipline and effort.

Hence the universal and unending struggle for freedom against the forces of enslavement both outside and within ourselves. We see it in political life; everyone struggling to run the country in such a way that they will get what they want, and being frustrated by the conflicting interests of other people. The same struggle for freedom is found in industrial life. We humans are so short-sighted that often we cannot understand that, by sacrificing our personal interests for the good of the community at large, we gain a freedom that only the community can give us.

When we think of freedom we usually think of having external conditions the way we want them, but there is an inner freedom of spirit which is the most important of all. We are enslaved by our selfish desires, we are entangled by material things so that we feel utterly unable to give fulfilment to the deep spiritual longings that we sometimes feel in our hearts.

One hears it said that among young people today there is a thirst for spiritual things, that they are dissatisfied with the materialism of life, and they want to break away from the structures of our highly organized society, to live a simple life where the deep spiritual elements of their personality can flourish. They make various attempts to achieve this, such as by opting out of the established order, forming various groups and communes, but usually ending up in frustration or being sucked back again into the establishment. Christianity they feel has nothing to offer. It is part of the establishment. Very well, it is, but it is more. Christianity is part of everything. Christ is the universal Saviour. It may take generations to change the establishment, but here and now Christianity offers freedom and it comes through contemplative meditation. It can be found in Buddhism, in Hinduism, in

Sufism and elsewhere but nowhere so clear and so strong as in Christianity.

Some people think they have examined Christianity and found it wanting but they have never made contact with its inner power. From the death and resurrection of Christ a great spiritual power has been released into the world and through contemplative meditation the Christian gradually opens his soul to its full receptive capacity in order to be filled with this power. This means progressive freedom from the bondage of ignorance and the bondage of passion, and entry into the vast, unbounded regions of the spirit. God is unbounded, unlimited freedom, and as the soul gets closer to him it shares in his freedom. It can turn to good all evils that happen to it. By reacting the right way to everything, everything plunges it deeper into this boundless freedom.

St John of the Cross drew a picture representing the Mount of Perfection. There were three pathways leading upwards. On the right was the path of an erring soul, a soul that was more concerned with earthly pleasures than with the things of God. It was a winding path, strewn with obstacles. It was wide at the beginning but got narrower as it advanced and eventually led off the mountain altogether. On the left was the path of an imperfect soul. This meant a soul that was interested indeed in spiritual things, but chiefly for the sake of the satisfaction it got out of them, looking for experiences and clinging to them. This path also was wide and winding, strewn with obstacles. It got narrower as it advanced and came to an end only halfway up the mountain. In the centre was the path of a perfect soul. This meant a person who had set his heart on God and was determined to let nothing get in the way of finding him. It started off straight and narrow but there were no obstacles and as it advanced it gradually widened out and eventually there was no path at all because the soul had been taken over by the Spirit of God and now shares in his freedom. "Here there is no path because for the just there is no law," said St John.

What holds so many people back from this spiritual freedom in spite of their good desires is that they are afraid to commit themselves. They may even think that commitment deprives them of freedom. As long as they are standing back considering various things that they could do, they feel they are free. Or if they do decide on something it is with the idea that if they do not like it they will pull out. But to commit themselves permanently to one thing is to exclude all the others, and this, they feel, is loss of freedom. And they feel that in concentrating on one thing they are missing many other experiences.

Freedom is given to be used. It is by commitment that we use it.

What good is our freedom unless we know how to make a decision? And if we try many things for a little while, pulling out as soon as we dislike them, what have we gained? Just a superficial knowledge of different things, but we have contributed nothing to the welfare of our fellow humans, and contributed nothing to our personal development. It is when difficulties arise in our chosen work and we face up to them and persevere in what we have started, turning to God for help, it is then that the finest qualities in our personalities are drawn out and developed. In fact it might be said it does not matter very much what we commit ourselves to as long as it is good in itself and we are capable of doing it. If we work in partnership with God, giving ourselves whole-heartedly to the work, it will be a means of spiritual growth and lead us into freedom of spirit.

16

Obedience

Just as freedom is earnestly sought after, so anything that would curb our freedom is strongly resisted. There is one virtue we find hard to understand because it seems to curb our freedom, that is the virtue of obedience. Having someone telling us what to do is repugnant to our innate sense of freedom. And yet it is impossible to get away from obedience.

Obedience is built into the nature of our society. When even two or three people are working together for a purpose, their only hope of success is by united effort. If they cannot achieve unity the group disintegrates, and unity can only be achieved when individuals adjust their personal desires to the common will of the group. This is obedience. True, each one contributes his personal opinions; they are discussed and may be accepted entirely, partially or not at all. Finally the group acts on majority agreement towards which each one has contributed something and may also have sacrificed something of his own opinions. This is the obedience of individuals to the group. We are prepared to make sacrifices of this kind because we know that some things we want can be achieved by united group effort, which coiuld not be achieved by ourselves individually. Many societies fail in their purpose because individuals refuse to let themselves be blended into a unity.

There are also societies that we must of necessity belong to, such as the family and the state. The same principles apply here. The state makes its laws and insists on their being obeyed. A little reflection enables us to realize that the common good of society is more to our advantage than the individual good we have to sacrifice for its sake. In general it can be said that taxes are worthwhile for the sake of public services. Traffic laws are worthwhile to avoid confusion on the roads. A police force is worthwhile to safeguard our lives and property. All these things impose restrictions on our personal freedom, but we submit to them for the sake of the advantages they bring us. This again is obedience: the submission of the individual to the common good as presented by lawful authority.

Authority is a focus for unity. In small groups it may be possible for the group as a whole to make all its decisions, although even here some kind of chairman will be needed. In large groups someone must be chosen to represent the society and direct it towards its purpose. Such a person is said to have authority but he must use it within the limits that the society itself has laid down. As universal agreement is almost impossible to achieve on many issues, the good of society demands that authority be obeyed even by those who do not agree with it.

I have said the above just to show that authority and obedience are an essential ingredient of human society. It would be outside my scope to go into the subject any further.

I would, however, like to say something about authority in the Church. Many people think that religion is just a private affair between oneself and God. It certainly is that but that is not all. Christ founded a Church and gave it a structure. We cannot have Christ without the Church, because Christ wants the Church. He told his apostles: "Go, therefore, and make disciples of all nations, baptizing them in the name of the Father and of the Son and of the Holy Spirit, teaching them to observe all that I have commanded you; and lo, I am with you always, to the close of the age." (Matthew 28:19-20)

In the practical administration of its affairs the Church can be as democratic as she wishes, but in its essential teaching concerning what to believe and how to behave, she must look to Christ and obey him only. And Christians must obey those human authorities that Christ has chosen to proclaim his teachings. This is where obedience hurts. Many people want to be free to get their own blend of Christianity directly from the Bible or from the theological writers that suit them. But that is not what Christ said. It is the apostles and their successors who have been commissioned by Christ to teach, and it is them we must obey. We think that this obedience curbs our freedom, but it only saves us from error. Error is slavery. It is the truth that makes us free, as Christ himself said.

The function of all authority is to give the security of a framework within which we can develop towards greater freedom. This framework saves us from evils and mistakes that would damage our progress. Civil authority saves us from the injustice of others so that we can freely develop our lives. Church authority saves us from anything that would lead us away from God, so that we are free to fulfil the purpose of our creation. Law only clears the way; it does not supply the power. This comes from love; our love and God's love working within us. Authority must not dominate our lives but safeguard our interests so that we can develop freely.

Connected with authority and obedience is the matter of spiritual direction, where a person freely accepts the guidance of another in order to be trained in the spiritual life. Some people object to this, saying that they want to develop from within and not to be given orders from without. But spiritual direction consists precisely in helping a person to develop from within. The director listens carefully to the disciple, gains an understanding of the way God is leading him and helps him along that way.

To think that one can direct oneself with the help of books is a mistake. What one reads in books cannot be applied to everyone, and a person can easily misinterpret what he reads in applying it to himself. No one is a judge in his own case. Or a person might say, "I follow my conscience; that keeps me safe". Yes, it saves one from sin but it does not save one from making mistakes. And a person can waste a lot of time and even give up the spiritual life entirely through not understanding it properly. Sometimes a person will even say, "I want to be free to make my mistakes and learn from them". But only too often we do not learn from our mistakes; we get caught up in them and persevere in them. And in any case a person should always seek the truth by the surest way because a freedom that leads to error ends in slavery whereas truth is the surest way to freedom.

The fact is that we are extremely self-centred and left to ourselves we turn everything, even God, to our own advantage. Our spiritual life can develop into a subtle form of self-glorification. We do what we want and think we are obeying God. But in order to find God we need to turn around in the opposite direction, to change our centre from self to God. We need help to do this. We are so buried in self that we need another person to pull us out. If we want to rely directly only on God we shall interpret God according to our own selfish desires. We shall pull him into the orbit of our own selfishness. It is quite different, though, when a person would gladly submit to a spiritual director and desires one but is unable to find a suitable one. Such a person can rest assured that God will provide the necessary guidance either by direct inspirations or by making use of circumstances.

It is a very normal thing that when a person wants to learn something he goes to a teacher and it is recognized that personal tuition has much to give that cannot be gained from books. So too with the spiritual life. It is God's plan to draw us to himself through the help of other people, and only when this fails will he make up for it directly himself. This master-disciple relationship exists in all the great religious traditions; for example, the *staretz* in the Russian Orthodox Church, the *guru* in Yoga, the *roshi* in Zen. In fact, in some other traditions the relationship is much more intimate than in Christianity. The disciple who submits himself to a *guru* has to be absolutely devoted to him and obey his every wish even in the smallest things. He must form an intimate soul-relationship with his *guru* and absorb his teachings without any opposition. Christianity does not ask for a dependence of this kind because it sees a spiritual director only as a representative of Jesus Christ. Christ is the real *guru* and the director's function is to stand to one side helping his disciple to surrender himself to the influence of Christ.

The question is often asked: Is a spiritual director necessary? At least for a Roman Catholic, and speaking in general, the answer is No. A Catholic has the living voice of Christ coming through in the clear teachings of his Church; he can ask advice from a priest at any time when he confesses his sins in the sacrament of Penance. In this way a person will often find a spiritual director almost without realizing it. While a disciple will usually follow the advice given by a director, he is not strictly bound to, unless the law of Christ or the Church is involved. And he is always free to change from one director to another.

17

Christian Poverty

The principal obstacles of the inflowing of God into our souls through contemplation are the disordered attitudes of our hearts and our disordered emotions and instincts. But material things also can be an obstacle not so much the things themselves as our attitude towards them. Hence the necessity of cultivating Christian poverty. When people think of poverty they usually visualize someone living in rags, undernourished, and with no place to live. That is not Christian poverty; that is destitution, and destitution is not an ideal to be aimed at; it is an evil to be remedied. Or they think of someone living in surroundings of filth and disorder. That is not Christian poverty, either. That is squalor; and squalor, too, is an evil to be remedied.

Christian poverty means having what is necessary for the welfare of mind and body, but no more. It can well be described as simplicity of life-style. Material things are intended to help us to get closer to God; insofar as they become a hindrance they should be discarded. That is the ideal, but a person sometimes has to live in circumstances of luxury and is not free to change them. In such cases detachment of heart is sufficient but it is easier said than done.

In order to develop a true spirit of Christian poverty the following points should be attended to:

(1) Do some work for the welfare of society. Most jobs contribute towards this end; but those who are wealthy and do not need to work for money have all the more reason to work for the welfare of the poor.

(2) Curb the desire for more and more money. It captures the mind and binds it to material things, holding it back from the spiritual. It is natural for a gifted person to achieve success in his work and earn big money, but if he finds ways and means of using his surplus money to promote the welfare of others he will be able to keep his heart detached from his wealth and his life directed towards God.

But poor people too can set their hearts on money, simply because they do not have enough of it. To be deprived of the necessities of life is a serious handicap to one's spiritual growth, and one needs strong faith and confidence in the providence of God to be able to cope with it. But for one who has this confidence what was a handicap becomes a blessing. The life-style most suited for Christian poverty is when a person can live in moderate comfort, without anxiety about his daily needs.

(3) It is important to know how to keep our needs reduced to a minimum. Material things have a way of dragging us down from the spiritual, and the fewer of them we need the freer we are to rise to the spiritual. This applies to ordinary household objects, the things we have in our sitting-room, our bedroom, our kitchen. We do not realize how much we are influenced by the mass media. We are bombarded by advertisements, many of them very subtle. They are specially geared to touch us on sensitive spots, the feeling that we are overweight, that we are tired and need a holiday, or that we could do with some labour-saving devices. The advertiser has so many suggestions as to how we could make our lives more convenient and more comfortable. We may think we are resisting these suggestions at the time; but they sink into us, and later on when we decide to buy something we think we are doing it on our own initiative, whereas it is the unconscious influence of advertisements previously seen. Thus we find ourselves getting cluttered up with things we do not really need and our freedom of spirit is injured. Hence it is a good thing to go through all our belongings from time to time and get rid of everything we do not really need. We shall be surprised at the feeling of freedom that comes to us as a result. But it is not an easy thing to do because we do cling to things. We find excuses, thinking "that might come in useful later on'; and so it might, but it is worthwhile to get rid of it all the same if we can manage without it.

Christian poverty, then, means simplicity of life; using material things to support our spiritual life yet knowing that too many of them would have the opposite effect.

18

Harmony in Detail

Referring again to the need for inner harmony in order to allow God to flow freely into us in contemplation, I have spoken of harmony of heart through virtue, and the corresponding harmony in our emotions and instincts, and the harmony that we should try to develop in regard to material things in general. But special consideration must be given to the manner in which certain things in our life need to be brought into line with the spirit.

First of all the body. It should be given the right amount of food, sleep, and exercise. Contemplation generally leads a person towards light eating, but vegetarianism is not essential. Many who practise it do so, not on account of contemplation, but as a protest against killing animals. And there are many who get over-interested in the study and practice of various diets in order, as they think, to eat only what is good for them and what helps the spirit. In reality they may be letting their minds get too absorbed in something material, and they can easily make mistakes. They are being guided by their discursive mind and not by their contemplation, and the discursive mind is not a sufficient guide. It is contemplation that gives a person the sensitivity to listen to his body. For the body know how to ask for what it needs, and if it is in a normal healthy condition its instincts can be trusted. It tells a person what to eat and it tells him when to stop. But people only too often fail to listen to the body because they lack the sensitivity that contemplation gives, or they are indoctrinated by what they read or hear about diets, or they submit to social pressures.

It is important also to give the body regular and sufficient sleep.

Irregular hours of sleep upset the rhythm of the body and disturb the calmness that is so necessary for contemplation. When a person is busy about his daily work he often does not realize he is tired, but as soon as he relaxes in order to meditate he finds himself going to sleep. Granted that one adopts a posture that keeps one alert but at the same time comfortable, it is best to concentrate on the meditation and take no notice whether one sleeps or not. Giving too much attention to fighting sleep is really a distraction while a person can be in genuine contemplation even though he is half asleep at the same time. Sometimes a person thinks he has been asleep when really he has been in a state of contemplation. He will usually know the difference by how he feels on coming out of it.

The body also needs exercise to keep it a fit instrument for the spirit. But when God takes the matter out of our hands by giving us illness, then he will draw us to himself through that very illness if we accept it from him. For our part, though, we must do what we can to keep the body in good working order.

In this regard there is one particular kind of exercise that deserves special mention. That is yoga exercise or what is known as *hatha yoga*. I am not referring now to any of the yoga systems of meditation or of developing extraordinary psychic powers but only to its system of physical exercises. These have a special value because they were developed with a view to attuning the body for meditation and they are just as helpful for Christian meditation as they are for any other kind. Unlike other forms of exercise, they do not aim at muscular development. They work on the internal organs of the body, on the glands, on the brain, the spine, the nervous system. They aim at promoting all-round health of body in a way that reacts on the mind as well, giving it a certain balance and calmness which disposes it for meditation. In former times saintly people sought to control their bodies by various forms of self-torture. To our minds such behaviour seems negative and destructive. While we recognize that the body needs to be subjected to discipline, we regard such treatment as injurious to its fitness for either work or prayer. *Hatha yoga,* however, is an excellent form of discipline for the body, and while it promotes calmness and relaxation it also increases its energy. Its benefits are especially noticeable as one gets older, as it keeps both body and mind in good condition.

One can understand easily enough how harmony of soul and body are valuable dispositions for contemplation, but when it comes to self-discipline as regards the clothes we wear and the room we sleep in, many people would think that these things are not important. Perhaps in a sense they are not important, yet as contemplation develops it penetrates into everything. It is said that genius is an infinite capacity for taking pains, and it is true also of contemplation that as it gets stronger it wants to express itself not only in the big important things but also down to the smallest detail. Nothing is too little for a great love. Bearing this in mind I want to say something on these matters of lesser importance.

Clothes are not only necessary to cover the body but also to express something of one's personality or function. When it is important for society to be able to recognize a person's function, a uniform is often worn, as in the case of policemen or priests. Then there is a philosophy of clothes by which one dresses to suit the occasion, whether it be at church, at business, at recreation or on the beach. Over and above these considerations, however, clothes express something more intimate about each individual, something of his inner attitude of mind. There would be endless variety of opinion as to what this might be in different cases. Even among contemplatives there will be different attitudes regarding clothes. Some will dress shabbily and carelessly in a spirit of detachment from worldly vanity. Others will dress in the most fashionable way in order to make religion seem modern and attractive.

Whatever might be said in favour of these attitudes, there is something more basic and more God-centred. God has his dwelling-place in our soul, not just as a Creator in his universe but as a friend who lives with his friend. Our bodies therefore can fittingly be called temples of God. Therefore they should be clothed in a manner worthy of this dignity. There is no use asking what this means in practice. This understanding comes intuitively from a person's awareness of God's presence in his soul.

Harmony should extend itself also to the environment in which we live, insofar as it is under our control, that is, our house, our sitting-room, our bedroom. Here it means keeping things clean and tidy. If harmony is right in every other sphere it is right here also. People say they have no time for these details because they are attending to more important things, but in fact it is these externals that betray the defects in our inner attitudes, and the self-discipline required to keep our room tidy and clean helps us to develop an orderly mind and strengthens our attachment to God.

19

The Light of Truth

Contemplative meditation produces its principal effects in our spiritual faculties, the intellect and the will, or as we also call them, the mind and the heart. To the mind it gives the light of truth and to the heart it gives love.

I want to say something now about the first of these. In contemplation truth is communicated, not to the thinking mind by means of ideas, but to the intuitive mind directly. You are not aware of receiving it but you know you have it by its effects. The intuitive mind is the silent mind, the passive mind, the unconscious mind. It is like the calm water of a lake in which the trees on the bank are perfectly reflected. Or like a sensitive photographic plate.

Truth is the harmony of mind with reality. If I say there is a table in a room and if in fact that is so, then my statement is true. If it is not so, my statement is false. There are people who think that truth is only in the mind, so that for me there is a table in the room but for you no table. That is called subjectivism. You cannot talk to a person who thinks like that. Fortunately there are not many of them. Instead of using the word 'reality' to describe truth one can use the word 'being' which means the same thing. Truth is the harmony of the mind with being. Now, in contemplation, when we go beyond all particular kinds of being (thoughts, images, feelings) we make direct contact with Being Itself which is the Source of all beings. By thus entering into harmony with the Source we develop an instinct for harmony with everything that comes from the Source. That is, we develop an instinct for harmony with all being, all reality. In other words, an instinct for truth.

Since truth is a relationship of our mind to the reality of God's universe and its laws, it follows that truth is objective and truth is one. God's creation is a reality, independent of our minds and we are either in harmony with it or we are not. Therefore contradictory opinions cannot both be true. A lady once objected to this, saying, "You say this glass is half full and I say it is half empty, and yet we are both right". She forgot that we were talking about different parts of the glass. But while truth is one, it is certainly many-sided. And some truths are so complicated that there seem to be an endless variety of aspects under which they can be considered. So when people have contrary opinions they are often just looking at different aspects of the same thing.

There is a story told about four blind men who went to the zoo to visit the elephant. On returning they were asked what the elephant was like. One man had put his arms round the elephant's leg and he said, "An elephant is like the trunk of a tree". Another had felt the animal's side and he said, "An elephant is like the sidewall of a house". Another caught hold of his trunk and said, "An elephant is like a hose". The fourth man held his tail and said, "An elephant is like a whip". What they all said was true as far as it went, but they only had partial knowledge and each one got a very inadequate and misleading idea of what the elephant was really like.

So, too, differences of belief among various religions are sometimes due to seeing different aspects of the same truth, sometimes to expressing the same truth in the language of different cultures. Or again they may involve direct contradictions, as when one religion derides exactly what another affirms. In view of such confusion of beliefs there are many who say that it does not matter what one believes as long as one lives a good life according to one's conscience. There is some truth in this but it can be extremely difficult to carry out in practice. It implies that a person has a great longing to find the truth concerning God and knows that by himself he is incapable of doing this. He will cry out for help, perhaps by such prayer as, 'O God, if you do exist, help me to find you'.

It is not only atheists and agnostics who are confused in their beliefs. Many Christians also. And because they think they understand things well, they lack the humility to see their mistakes. They enjoy their intellectual interest in religion and they do not ask for God's help. It is well to remember, then, that to follow one's conscience in sincerity is not as easy as it sounds. And, apart from this, it does matter what one believes. A good conscience saves from sin but it does not save from mistakes. Truth is freedom;

error is bondage. It is important, then, that we should attain to the full truth that God has given us for the purpose of directing our lives towards him. This is where contemplation helps immensely. It guides us to the truth and it gives us a deeper appreciation of it.

Contemplation of itself does not communicate new truths to us. If we learn something in contemplation that we could not have known otherwise, that is called revelation, and it is difficult to be sure if it is genuine. Such knowledge could come from our own unconscious minds or from the evil spirit. Even when it comes from God we can easily misinterpret its meaning. St John of the Cross advises us to ignore all such revelations. Then if they come from ourselves or from the devil they will do us no harm. If they come from God they will produce their effect in our souls independently of any reaction of ours, so that we are still right to ignore them. If God speaks to us and tells us to do something, unless it is obviously something we ought to do, we should seek and obey the advice of a wise spiritual director.

But contemplation does guide our thinking mind towards the discovery of truth, especially religious truth. If a person is poorly instructed in his religion, contemplation will make him realize this. It will guide him in his search for suitable books. It will give him a humble attitude in his reading, so that he does not trust in his own intelligence but leans on God to give him a right understanding of what he reads. Also it will give him an ability to discern anything that is not quite true. Even books written by outstanding Christian scholars can sometimes be at fault, their own personal opinions getting in the way of the true teachings of Christ and the Church. Contemplation also gives a person a deeper appreciation of religious truths, such as the evil of sin, the meaning of redemption and of the Eucharist, the love of God for us, the reality of hell. In a word, contemplation will enable a person to see things more and more with the mind of Christ and feel things with the heart of Christ.

The light of contemplation is not confined to religious matters; it penetrates every aspect of our lives. The practical business of day-to-day life, the continual minor decisions that have to be made; all these come under the guiding light of contemplation with the result that a great calmness and peace envelop our life, and no matter what else we might be doing, our heart is being drawn to God.

When the light of God is clear in us everything is worthwhile and even difficult things seem easy. It is not by mental struggles that we get this light, but rather by not getting in God's way by our own activity, by allowing our minds to be calm, silent and attentive, so as not to offer any obstacle to the inflowing of that heavenly light that so transforms our lives.

20

Love

As contemplation illuminates the mind with the light of truth so also it enkindles in the heart the fire of love. This love is not to be thought of as emotional in the ordinary sense. It is something deep in the spirit, strong, sensitive, penetrating. At times it might not be felt at all but is a hidden power that shows itself in action. At other times it is felt as a warmth in the region of the heart or even as a flame of fire, painful yet sweet.

In contemplation the will or heart is in direct contact with Infinite Being and it is attracted by its goodness. Goodness is just another aspect of being. It is the attractiveness of being. In this contact the heart is enkindled with desire for God who is the Source of its being, and this desire can develop to an intense longing. It opens up the soul and deepens its capacity to receive God more and more. God thus communicates more and more of his love to the soul, so that the soul wants to communicate what God has given it. It wants to radiate love. This is known as the love of goodwill, whereas the longing just spoken of is called the love of desire. This, too, when centred on God is a genuine form of love and very important for the development of contemplation. The more we desire God the stronger our link with him and the more he can give us. And of all that he gives us there is nothing greater than the love of goodwill.

This love of goodwill shows itself in the first place towards God himself. We give ourselves to him; we surrender our lives to him so that he can live in us and through us. However, God has given us a very practical way of showing our love for him, by telling us to love other people. He even tells us that he takes as being done to himself what we do to others.

We can consider love basically as a sharing of being. We are all defective in being; we are not sufficient for ourselves. God is all-sufficient, but at the same time he wants us to support one another and share with one another. We all need this support; we all feel the need to be loved. To know that we are loved by God is the greatest support and comfort, especially when life is difficult. But we need human love as well; if we do not get it we wilt and fade.

We need to feel that we are accepted and approved of, that at least there are some people who believe in us. It is true that God's love can make up for the loss of all other love, and more than make up for it, but such detachment can only be achieved at the cost of much struggle and prayer. Many people, however, go the wrong way about getting themselves loved. They go looking for it and grasping at it and trying to take possession of people's hearts. But people simply run away from them. You cannot command love. The only way to find love is by giving love. "Where there is no love", says St John of the Cross, "put love and you will find love". It should be our aim, then, to radiate among people the love that we draw from God in contemplation.

The love we give to people is more than natural human love. Our natural love is very tarnished by selfishness and very unreliable but it is transformed by the inflowing of love that comes from God. This divine love does not overwhelm our human love and take its place. On the contrary, it enters into it and develops all that is best in it. Human love is at its very best when it is enlivened by the love that comes from God. And this divine-human love finds what it seeks in every human heart, for in every human heart there is an image of God. God has expressed something of his own beauty in every individual and it is different in each one. Of all the innumerable millions of people God has created no two are the same, which means that God loves each of us as an individual. This divine image in people cannot be seen directly, at least not in this life. To some extent it shows through the personality, yet there are cases in which an evil personality entirely obscures it, but faith gives us certainty that it exists in everyone.

Because all bear this divine image God loves everyone, even the greatest sinner; and it is for the same reason that he wants us to love everyone. When people have lost God's friendship through sin God still loves them in order to make them his friends. And when we see evil in people we still love them with a desire to see them cured of the evil that is in them so that God's image might shine in them more clearly. To love people means having an attitude of goodwill towards them but it does not necessarily mean cultivating their companionship. We can easily be too confident of our ability to help people when in fact they might have a bad influence on us. Even though they need help, we might not be the right people to help them. We should pray and possibly seek advice before deciding to help someone who might have a bad influence on us. We must not act on our own initiative however well-intentioned, but must be guided by God and sent by him. And sometimes his guidance will be to have nothing to do with a certain person, no matter how much he might need help.

While love is basically a radiation of goodwill towards people, there are innumerable ways in which it can express itself, and about three of these ways in particular I would like to say something. These are understanding, patience, and right speech.

The first is understanding. Understanding is the guiding light of love, and it is sad to see so much love being misdirected through lack of understanding. Giving presents is one example. People often embarrass their friends by giving them the wrong kind of presents. They are thinking more of showing their own love than of what their friend would appreciate. Their pleasure in loving is more important to them than the pleasure of their friend in receiving the gift. They feel their friend ought to be pleased with what they think is right. A curious poisoning of love by selfishness! A man once received a present of a horse and his comment was, "I do not like presents that have to be fed".

In the life of St Therese of Lisieux it is recorded that while in a very delicate state of health she was served food that disagreed with her. Being a saint, she would not dream of complaining, but she had three blood-sisters in the convent who saw what was happening and were very distressed by it. They were powerless, however, to do anything about it because the prioress had her own views as to how Therese should be treated. Then one of her own sisters became bursar and had charge of providing the food and she said to herself, "Now at last Therese will get the food that suits her". But she gave her the food that she herself liked, and she had a strong, healthy appetite. The result was that Therese suffered as much as ever from unsuitable food, with the added tragedy that it was all done to her through misdirected love, a love without understanding.

There is another example from the life of the same saint. When Therese's illness was more advanced and she was very weak, she would sit in a wheel-chair in the garden, trying with great effort to finish the last pages of her autobiography. The sisters, returning from the hayfield, would pass by where she was and would think, "Poor Therese, I am sure she must be lonely and would like a chat". And they would exhaust her with their well-meant conversation, thinking they were doing her an act of kindness. Again, a lack of understanding. Something similar often happens in hospital with patients too ill to cope with visitors.

Some people have a special gift of understanding; they seem to know exactly what is needed in a given situation. Yet there is much that everyone can do to acquire this valuable quality, and it can all be summed up in three words: Listen to people.

We need to listen to people, not just with our mind but with our heart. Not with the detached professional skill of a psychiatrist, tabulating in his mind the nature of their complaint, but rather with the insight given by love. In order to achieve this one needs to get out of oneself and enter into the feelings of another; to get away from one's preconceived ideas of what answers are needed, and to know how to adapt to what is required in this unique situation. It is so easy to say, "Now listen to me and I will tell you what to do", when it is we who should listen to the other person and guide him in finding the answer to his own problem, or ourselves come to understand what is needed, not in theory, which we know well enough, but in this practical situation.

But it is not enough to listen to people in order to love them with understanding; we must listen to God also. This we do in contemplation; and as the habit of contemplation grows stronger it begins to underlie all our activities, so that while we are dealing with people God is guiding us in what we say and do. But in order that this be so we must have a basic trust in God's guidance and not in our own ability.

A second way in which love expresses itself is by patience. It is easy to love when we get pleasure out of loving, and this pleasure can easily become selfish, tarnishing the purity of our love. To love people in spite of the irritation they cause us requires a purer and more steadfast love. Some people we love and hate at the same time; we love them because they are good friends or perhaps even members of our family, yet sometimes we find ourselves having feelings of hatred towards them because of various ways in which they irritate us. If we are to continue to love them we must be willing to suffer these irritations without complaining and even cheerfully. We sometimes like to correct our friends and we think it is for their own good but in reality it is to stop them from behaving in a way that irritates us. We all have our imperfections, our defects of character, our shortcomings that at times hurt and annoy other people. Sometimes we are not even aware of them.

When we are so aware we find that often we are not able to change them. So when we cannot make ourselves perfect we should not try to make other people perfect for our convenience.

When we are face to face with a person whom it is difficult to love there is no time to think of the reasons why we ought to love him. The only thing to do is to allow goodness and kindness and gentleness to flow from us and not even give a thought to the things that annoy us. It is contemplative meditation that makes a person sufficiently alert to be able to do this. Even when there is no loving response from the other person we can still go on loving. Although we naturally desire to receive a return of love, we are not dependent on this because we are drawing our love from that inexhaustible source of love which is God.

A third expression of love can be called right speech. I understand this as referring to how we talk about people who are not present. There is nothing we like talking about so much as other people. This is quite normal because there is nothing in the world so interesting as other people. Look at an average newspaper and you will see that what it has to say about animals, plants, machines and heavenly bodies is very little in comparison with what it says about people. But unfortunately in talking about people we are too much inclined to criticize them. Even if we do not actually criticize we speak about them in a way that shows them up as being in some way inferior to ourselves. This is probably due to our own feelings of insecurity and our need to convince ourselves of our personal value, or simply our pride. We like to feel, often subconscously, that we are just a little better than others, and we like the people we are talking to to get the same impression.

That is not the way of love. In fact it is against a basic principle of human living, namely, that good should be proclaimed and evil kept hidden. Good should be proclaimed and made known as much as possible, in order that its influence may spread and be a source of inspiration for others; but evil should be kept hidden lest its influence might lead others to evil. Some would say that evil should be made widely known in order that it might be corrected and people might be warned against it. It is true that evil should be made known, but only to those people who are in a position to correct it, and only those should be warned against it who are in serious danger of being affected by it. On the whole, the welfare of society is far better served by publicizing what is good rather than what is evil. And yet by some strange quirk in our nature, good news is not nearly as attractive as bad news, provided, of course, that the bad news does not affect ourselves. And so the mass media daily give us stories of all kinds of crime and warfare and very little, in comparison, of the noble deeds of good men and women.

There is little we can do as individuals to change the tone of the mass media because it would mean changing the mentality of a society that has largely lost its appreciation of noble and spiritual ideals, but there is a lot we can do in our own conversation to diminish evil and increase what is good. It requires an attitude of humility by which we are ready to admire what is good in people and make excuses for their shortcomings. I once knew a man with whom I had many conversations, often about other people. During our conversations he never gave me the impression of going out of his way to praise people, but afterwards, in reflecting on our conversation, I found that I was left with a higher opinion of the people we had been talking about. That is what happens when we love the people we talk about even though they might be our enemies.

Love expresses itself differently according to different relationships, whether it be that of husband and wife, parents and children, brothers and sisters, intimate friends or mere casual acquaintances. But in every human relationship there should be love, even though it might only need to express itself in a kindly word and a pleasant manner. It should be present in the contacts of business life and in handling the problems of industrial life as well as in the complicated diplomacy of politics.

What hope is there of love dominating the hard-headed world of business if it does not exist in the seed-ground of the family? It is sad to say that many children grow up without ever having experienced the warmth and security of true love. A medical doctor was driving his car in London when a man thumbed a ride. The doctor gave it to him but was soon sorry he had done so as the man showed signs of becoming aggressive and violent. The doctor, however, remained calm and spoke to the man with kindness and gentleness. Imagine his surprise when after a few moments the man broke down and cried. "Never," he said, "until this moment has anyone ever spoken a kind word to me". Is it any wonder that people would turn to crime when they have never known what it is to be loved. When love grows weak in human society all kinds of evils develop; and love grows weak when society turns away from God who is the source of love.

There is not very much an individual can do to bring back love into society as a whole, but God has care of his children even when they forget him, and he will never allow love to die out in the world. Ever since that mighty act of love took place when Christ died on Calvary, a great power of love has been released into the world that will never fail. Although evil may seem widespread and dominant the goodness and beauty of love is present also, hidden perhaps but powerful, and in many ways it comes to the surface. Every saint is a manifestation of the Spirit of love in the world, and there are more saints among us than many realize. A lady was once talking to Pope Pius XI saying how sad she was that evil was gaining such power in the world. "Do not worry", replied the pope, "there is a saint in every street".

That remark of his brings our attention back again to the individual. It is through individuals that God communicates his love to the world. Love is contagious, "Where there is no love, put love and you will find love", says St John of the Cross. Love has its source in God and it seeks the hearts of those who are receptive to it. Through them it reaches out to others, gradually breaking down the barriers of hatred and pride and bringing happiness to many people who had lost their way because they did not know what love is.

21

Auto-Suggestion

Contemplation gives us spiritual light and power that can bring us into the closest union with God. But it will not produce this effect in us unless we do our part by making whatever effort is needed towards this end. It is important, then, that we know how to use our natural powers to the best advantage, but even while doing this we need to keep leaning on God for guidance and support. In living a spiritual life there are many things that call for a firm resolution on our part, the most basic being the desire for holiness itself. Also the organization of our daily life in such a way as to leave time for spiritual reading and contemplation. Then there are certain faults that we need to struggle against and certain virtues to be practised. We need to pray for God's help about all this, but we also need personal effort.

We all have experience of having made good resolutions and broken them, and sometimes after a few failures we have given up entirely. One reason for this is that we do not bring the full power of our mind and will to bear on carrying out our resolutions. We sometimes complain of not having much will-power yet it is not really will-power that is lacking but rather a deep and clear-sighted appreciation of our motives and a certainty that our motives are the most suitable ones. Sound motives, clearly seen and deeply appreciated enable the will to carry out a difficult undertaking with comparative ease, whereas if a person through sheer will-power forces himself to do something that he knows is right yet is very much against the trend of his thoughts and feelings, he causes himself much pain and nervous tension. Over a space of time this might lead to a nervous breakdown. We can indeed fear for a person's welfare when with a strong will he forces himself to do something without trying to bring his thoughts and feelings into harmony with his will.

In order to bring the full power of our mind to bear on carrying out our resolutions there is more involved than just bringing our thoughts and feelings into line with our will. There is the question of how to utilize the power of our unconscious mind. A large area of our mind is outside the reach of our conscious control and yet it has great influence on our behaviour. It is said that the mind is like an iceberg of which only one-tenth can be seen above the water. Before our first parents sinned against God it is likely that there was no such thing as an unconscious mind. The human mind was then bathed entirely in the light of God, but sin caused it to sink into darkness, with only a small area remaining in the light of consciousness. Yet this unconscious area is very powerful as the following illustrations will help to explain.

Imagine a house with a large hallway inside the front door and a stairs at the further end leading down to a basement. For some reason messages are continually being handed in at the front door and there is a porter in the hallway whose duty it is to put a label on each message and file it away in the basement. If he puts on the right label the message is correctly filed and is available for use at any time, but if he puts on the wrong label the message gets lost in the filing system, not being available for use when needed. When this happens to a considerable number of messages disorder is created in the system.

The hallway represents the conscious human mind. The messages being handed in are the impressions and experiences continually coming to us through the senses, especially the things we see and hear. The porter is our conscious *ego* which reacts to every experience. If we react the right way, the Christlike way, we are putting the right label on the experience and it goes to its proper place in the filing system which is our unconscious mind. As more and more similar experiences, accompanied by our right reactions, sink into the unconscious mind, they gather strength there and are available when needed in order to cope with a difficult situation. But if the wrong label gets attached to an experience, that is if we react to it in a negative way such as resentment, hatred, irrational anger or fear, or any other such disorderly feelings, these reactions sink into our unconscious mind together with the experiences that caused them. In the course of time they gather strength, but because the labels are not correct they are lost in the filing system and cannot be used for a good purpose. Nevertheless as they get stronger they demand an outlet. And since of their very nature they are incapable of a constructive outlet for the welfare of the personality, they eventually break through into consciousness, causing disturbance of mind and even of body. In this way various kinds of neurotic behaviour develop and even physical illnesses. This process of things developing in our unconscious mind goes on continually, for better or for worse. We cannot stop it; all we can do is try to make sure that what develops is for our good and not for our harm.

But while we cannot stop this process we can make use of it and direct it to a purpose of our own choice. If there is some particular thing that we want, we can deliberately send down to our unconscious mind positive reactions concerning it, so that these will gradually develop strength and eventually break through into consciousness to give us what we want. This is how we use the full power of our mind, conscious and unconscious, to carry out our resolution or to get what we want. Before we begin to do this we should make sure that what we want is according to God's will. To do wrong with only conscious will-power is bad enough, but to do wrong with total will-power is very much worse. In chapter seven I have offered guidance for discerning God's will in making decisions.

Having assured ourselves as far as possible that what we want is God's will, we then see ourselves as already having it. In our mind's eye we form a clear idea or mental picture of what we want. We recognize the difficulties involved in getting it but we believe they can be overcome, and we see our objective as something attractive and desirable. We hold this idea steadily before our minds day after day so that our desire for it increases. We allow ourselves no anxiety or fear that we might not get it but rather enjoy it in our minds as though we already had it. This idea, together with the certainty that it will be realized, sinks into our unconscious mind and gathers strength there, and eventually comes through with power to give us what we want.

How can it do this? It does not seem to make sense that merely desiring a thing in a clear and positive way is enough to give it to us. Yet such a desire can, indeed, achieve this, and for two reasons. First, it makes us aware of opportunities that we should otherwise overlook. We are surrounded by opportunities that we do not see, but this clear-sighted and confident desire, when it develops power in our unconscious mind, gives us an uncanny sensitivity for seizing opportunities of getting what we want, or makes the keeping of a resolution so much part of our nature that it would cost us a real effort to do otherwise. The second reason is that because we are desiring something that we know to be God's will, our desire is really an implicit prayer that God would grant it to us. When we direct the full power of our mind and will towards doing what pleases God we are totally working in harmony with God. And God also works in harmony with us so that his power which governs the universe is at our disposal to give us what we want. As Jesus said, "If you abide in me and my words abide in you, ask whatever you will, and it shall be done for you". (John 15:7). This truth can also be expressed on a non-religious level by the saying that if you act in harmony with nature, nature will support you.

These principles of autosuggestion can be applied to any purpose we want to achieve. We simply get a clear and attractive picture of what we want and feed our minds with it. Suppose you apply it to the desire for holiness. You first free your understanding of holiness from false elements, ideas which make it unattractive and even repulsive. For the most part we are not called to be geniuses of holiness like the great saints but simply to be holy within our own limited capacity. And we are not expected to be religious fanatics like some people who have the name of being holy but really are mentally unbalanced. Holiness requires no more of us than to live very ordinary human lives, but with our hearts filled with a great love for God which gradually comes to us through contemplation, and with a great love for other people, which is the overflow of our love for God. Having thus come to see holiness as something attractive, we feed our mind day by day with this idea of loving God and loving people ever more and more, and because we are doing this with the awareness that holiness is God's gift which we are humbly asking him to give us, we are opening out our unconscious mind as though it were a yawning abyss, wide and deep, calling out to be filled by God. Thus we are combining personal psychological effort with humble prayer for God's grace. We are utilizing the total power of our mind, conscious and unconscious, to beg of God the gift that we seek. Such prayer is very powerful to obtain our request.

We can bring this power of auto-suggestion to bear also on more detailed and earthly matters. Suppose you are in the habit of over-eating and putting on too much weight and you want to reduce your weight. The first thing is to make sure that what you want is God's will. So you must examine your motive. Do you merely want to appear more attractive to the eye so that people will praise us for our good looks? This motive could very easily be sheer vanity and selfishness, although not necessarily always, as when a woman makes herself attractive in order to have a good spiritual influence on someone else. But if our motive is in fact sefish, then God is not on our side, but we can still develop the power of our unconscious mind and it makes the offence against God all the worse. We may achieve immediate success in getting what we want but eventually it ends in worse disorder. The case of Hitler would seem to be a good example.

But to come back to the case I have mentioned, reducing weight. It has been said that a man is at his wisest at sixty, but unfortunately when he has most to give to others he begins to deteriorate physically and this can often be due in part to over-eating. Therefore if a person resolves carefully to control his diet in order that his body will be a fit instrument for doing God's work as long as possible, this motive is certainly pleasing to God and he can safely bring the power of his unconscious mind to bear on carrying out such a resolution. The next step is to get a clear mental picture of oneself, light and agile, able to move about easily to do God's work, and to keep this attractive picture before one's mind day after day. It gradually gains power in the unconscious mind so that the necessary discipline to achieve this object, far from being an unpleasant duty, becomes an enjoyable hobby.

Just as in prayer there is a development from discursive through the prayer of simplicity to contemplation, so in the practice of auto-suggestion there is a similar development. In the beginning we have to think out our motives and carefully shape our purpose into an attractive idea or mental picture and deliberately keep recalling it to mind over a period of time, but after a while the whole process becomes simplified in our mind so that we can take it all in at a single glance, and eventually it gets so drawn into our contemplation that we forget about it entirely, and the contemplation itself controls the process and gives us what we desire.

22

Making Sacrifices: Detachment

In contemplation we open our souls to the attraction of God. He draws us to himself as the Source of our being and as the Redeemer who has saved us from our sins. While we may succeed during a short period of contemplation in surrendering ourselves to this attraction, no sooner have we gone back to the activities of daily life than other attractions begin to assert themselves, things that take a grip on our affections and make us less inclined to turn to God.

These things may not be bad in themselves; in fact they may be very good in themselves, but they cause a certain disorder in our lives and in our feelings that gets between us and God. It might be a want of discipline and a giving in too much to the moods of the moment. It might even be that we spend too much time doing kind acts for other people so that we have no time left to set aside directly for God. Christ spent the days of his public life in the midst of people but he spent whole nights alone in prayer to his heavenly Father. If we cannot spend nights in prayer we must find some time for it during the day, and this may mean having to leave out certain good works. Another thing that easily distracts us from God is human friendship. Friendship can be a powerful influence in our lives, either to lead us to God or to hold us back from him. Sometimes we think a friendship is leading us to God because we pray with our friend or share spiritual thoughts with him, and yet all this might be merely a cover for selfish attachment.

Through our contemplation God gradually shows us the things that are holding us back from him, at the same time urging us to sacrifice them for his sake. There are some people who immediately give God what he asks, paying no attention to their own feelings; these quickly advance to union with God. But most people put up quite a struggle before they finally give in to God. In many ways they try to evade the urgings of God's grace. They try to convince themselves that God is not really asking for a sacrifice. There is nothing wrong in what they are doing, it has many advantages, it is helping other people. Yet underneath all their reasonings is the voice of conscience communicating God's request.

To keep on weighing up reasons for and against only confuses the mind all the more; the correct thing to do is to leave the matter in the hands of God and to continue with one's contemplation. Thus the light of God in us gets stronger until we see quite clearly that God is asking us for a sacrifice. Even then we may continue to struggle, telling ourselves that we simply are not able to do it. But the grace of contemplation will help us over this obstacle also if we trust in this grace and not in our own reasonings. There is a final obstacle which is perhaps the most difficult of all to overcome. We know God is asking for something, we know that with his help we can do it, but we do not want to do it. It is the obstinacy of our will that does not want to submit. An obstinate will can resist all reasonings and can even resist all grace. In a way it is fortunate for us that we are weak-willed, it means that we are capable of changing. If we make a decision with complete knowledge and the full power of our will, it would be practically impossible to change it, but that is most unlikely to happen in the present weak state of our human nature. Even when we find ourselves refusing to give God what he wants there is still something in us that wants to give in to him. God can work on this element of docility in us in order to get what he wants, provided we keep up our meditation.

While it is very important to give God what he asks of us, we must be careful not to imagine he is asking things when he is not. When we are in doubt we should stop thinking about the matter and leave it to God. Some people are afraid of enjoying themselves and when they are enjoying something they begin to think they ought to sacrifice it for God. Such people need to learn how to enjoy themselves for love of God. As long as we are doing what God wants us to do it is right that we should enjoy it. God has so arranged things that if we put ourselves wholeheartedly into the doing of our duty we shall get considerable pleasure from it. It is the spirit in which we do things that makes all the difference between being happy in our work and being miserable. Even hard, disagreeable work is transformed when we offer it as a gift of love to God. And if we keep our amusements in their proper place, without allowing them to interfere with more important duties, we can then enjoy them with a clear conscience. And in the midst of our enjoyments we should raise our hearts to God in frequent thanksgiving. Where the spirit of sacrifice shows is in the way we discipline our lives, doing everything at the right time, giving it proper care and attention, and observing suitable moderation in everything.

Sometimes people are frightened of giving God what he asks because they think that if they give him one thing he will ask for something else and eventually he will take everything and there will be nothing left. Obviously this is not true because God knows our needs and is only too willing to provide for them. What he wants to cure us of is our selfish clinging to things. When we learn how to enjoy his gifts in simplicity of heart and appreciation of his love in giving them, then he will give them to us in abundance. In order fully to enjoy God's gifts we need to be detached from them.

It can be hard to understand this. How can you enjoy something if you are detached from it? Does not detachment mean being aloof and disinterested? To enjoy, one must be involved. This is a common misunderstanding. To say someone is detached gives a picture of someone who lives in the clouds, unconcerned with what goes on around him, cold and indifferent to the problems of others. But this picture is entirely false. The detached person is the one who is truly involved and fully in touch with reality. This needs some explanation.

Detachment means not clinging to anything in a selfish way. The selfish person does not see things as they really are; he sees them only as they affect him in a pleasant or unpleasant way, and he misses their real worth. Because of his clinging he is influenced by fear lest he lose what he has or by an anxiety to gain what he has not. Thus his attention is diverted to the future and he misses much of the value of what is actually present. In fact, most of our attachments carry us either into the past or into the future. We daydream about the past, reliving happy moments that are gone, or feeling guilty about the mistakes we have made and the troubles we have brought on ourselves. Or we look forward to the future, living our holidays in anticipation or the renewal of our contact with dear friends, or what is more frequently the case, being afraid of the misfortunes that might befall us, such as losing our money, our health or our friends.

All such preoccupation with past or future draws away our vital energy from the present, and since the present moment is the only point at which we are in touch with reality, it means that we are not fully giving ourselves to life as it is. Life is like a wheel and as it revolves it touches the ground only at a single point which is continually changing. Or it is like a river, and we are watching the waters flowing past. The future is continually flowing into the present and away into the past. If we want to keep in touch with the present we must be letting it flow away all the time. If we try to go after it when it has past we miss the new experience that has come into the present. Or one can say that life is like climbing a ladder. We use each step in order to get to the top but we must leave each step behind in order to get to the next. So, too, we must let life keep changing and adapt ourselves to each new situation if we are to keep in contact with reality.

Although in theory the present moment is just a point of time, in fact our present life can contain many elements that have a certain relative permanence. Our present job remains the same for some time; so too the place where we live. Our friends, too, may stay with us over a considerable period. Therefore if we are enjoying our present life, as it is only right that we should, it is nevertheless possible to become attached to it. This shows if an unexpected change comes and has an upsetting effect on us. We are miserable at having to let go what we so much enjoyed and are longing to cling on to it.

Thus the question is, how can one remain detached when life is pleasant and enjoyable? And the answer is, by being interested in the enjoyable things and not in one's own enjoyment of them. Be interested in your home, in your job, in your friends, and above all in your God, but not in yourself. Pleasure is like a condiment that we use with food to make it more palatable, such as sugar, salt, pepper, sauce. But we should never think of making a meal of condiments only. So, too, when we are enjoying the good things of life, it is these things we should be thinking of and simply allowing the pleasure to come to us as a by-product without focusing our attention on it. This is just another way of saying, be unselfish in our enjoyments. If we cultivate this outgoing, unselfish attitude, spending ourselves joyfully in the service of our home, our job and our friends, and doing it all as a gift to the God who gave us all these things, then when something is taken away we do not find ourselves wanting to cling on to it, but instead we are ready to give ourselves to the new experience that comes in its place.

Everything in life is a gift from God. Even though sometimes it might be unpleasant and cause us real pain, if we accept it willingly as a gift from one who loves us and respond whole-heartedly to whatever demands it makes on us, we shall discover within it a hidden value and beauty and we shall usually find ourselves enjoying what at first sight seemed repulsive. But in order that this can happen, as soon as one thing is taken away from us, we must immediately turn our attention to what has come in its place. Indeed, as soon as we know that something is going to be taken away from us, instead of bewailing our loss we should turn our minds in joyful anticipation to the thought of what God is going to give us in its place. We need not say there is nothing in its place. Life does not stop. There is always something if we open our eyes to see it.

I heard of a lady in Australia who lived alone in a flat. She had a hobby of collecting little ornaments, figures of various kinds, of funny little men or children or angels. She enjoyed searching for these things and arranging them tastefully in her flat. They became to her like friends and she loved them. She also was in the habit of practising regular meditation, and eventually God began to show her that this hobby was getting between her and him. The thought of this upset her and she began to argue against it. It was such a good hobby, there was something so innocent about it. It kept her from worse things, from loneliness and depression and perhaps from seeking more dangerous amusements. Her meditation became more difficult, her heart was not in it, but at least she kept it up and kept asking God for help. That was what saved her. She could so easily have given up meditation but she did not. Then one day quite suddenly, almost without giving it a thought and without any struggle, she got rid of all her ornaments. How she disposed of them I was not told. And to her amazement, instead of the sense of loss that she had feared, she experienced a delightful sense of freedom. It was as though she had been bound by chains and now they were broken and she was free. And when she went back to her meditation it was as though God was waiting to welcome her in a way she had never known him before. A region of her heart that had previously been closed was now open and God was able to fill that empty space. I do not know how her life developed afterwards, but it could very well have happened that when her heart had become detached from these ornaments and firmly rooted in God, she could have gone back to them again in a more moderate way without letting her heart get absorbed in them, sharing them with God and even enjoying them more than ever.

The basic thing a person needs to remember about detachment and the sacrifices that lead to it, is that it is a way to greater freedom, greater union with God and greater enjoyment of life.

23

Effects on the Imagination and Body

Contemplation is known as a prayer of the heart because it comes through the contact of our heart, that is our will, with God. Our intellect also is involved, not in an active thinking way but in a passive, intuitive way. We refer to it as the intuitive mind. The imagination is a faculty we do not need in contemplation but it is difficult to get away from it because it is so much part of the natural working of our mind. I have already spoken about how the imagination troubles our contemplation by distractions and wandering thoughts. We are likely to suffer from these at any stage of our spiritual life. St Teresa of Avila was already far advanced in prayer when she still sometimes suffered from distractions. She once complained about this to our Lord and he said to her, "Teresa, you are not in heaven yet".

As discursive meditation becomes simplified it helps us to quieten the imagination. So also does the use of a mantra. But at times mental pictures arise in contemplation which are not distractions and are different from the usual wandering thoughts. They could be of any kind but often they represent scenes of natural beauty, woodlands, fields and rivers, mountains, blue sky and white clouds. Or perhaps a tunnel with light at the end of it.

Also colours, especially blue or yellow. Or simply a beautiful atmosphere of light. They rise up from the unconscious mind where contemplation is taking place and instead of distracting they hold a person in contemplation. They are like God-given mantras. I call them "offshoot" images because they seem to be offshoots of contemplation, that is, effects produced in the imagination by contemplation. But they are only helpful as long as a person does not start thinking about them. Sometimes they might be very interesting and attractive and one might be inclined to turn one's attention to them and begin to wonder what they mean. But this would stop the contemplation. It is all right to be aware of them, as when you are talking to one person you are aware that there is another person in the room. But all the time your attention must go beyond them to the Infinite.

Sometimes God uses these images to teach a person, usually by way of showing him a fault that needs correction, or the correct way of reacting in some situation, or simply giving him light on some spiritual truth. But here also the same rule holds: he must not start thinking about any of this. When we feel we have got some light from God there is a great temptation to start reflecting on it and thinking how to put it in practice; but this would only stop our contemplation. While we are in contemplation we must let God do his work in us and keep out of it ourselves. Whatever teaching he gives us will remain with us after the contemplation is over and then we can think about it.

It can also happen that while we are in a state of contemplation God himself will activate our thoughts and imagination so that we consciously think of him and talk to him and praise him. For example, he might lead us to keep company with him in scenes of his passion or inspire us to pray for people who are in need of help. But this is not discursive prayer. We are not doing it on our own initiative. It is God who is doing it in us and through us, and therefore it is part of our contemplation.

However, the very fact that God needs to use our imagination in order to help us can in itself be a sign that our imagination is not fully attuned to the spirit. As we advance in contemplation over a period of time the imagination tends to quieten down and the action of God takes place more purely in the spirit. People sometimes feel a little envious when, at meditation meetings, they hear other people talking about the interesting mental pictures that have come to them in contemplation, whereas they themselves never have anything but a steady blankness of mind. In fact this latter is a better state; God is communicating with them in a purely spiritual way. They are practising more completely a prayer of faith and they can be very happy in this state because it brings great peace with it and the knowledge that such faith is most pleasing to God.

Not only does contemplation produce effects in the imagination, it also produces them in the body. Sometimes a tingling sensation in the hands or feet, a burning sensation in the hands, a feeling that the body is getting heavy or getting light or swelling, a feeling that one is being drawn deep down as into a vortex, or that one is floating or that one is being drawn up out of oneself; or sometimes a feeling of being cold or being hot. None of these feelings is of any importance. None has any special significance. They are merely ways in which contemplation happens to be affecting the body. But they do indicate that the body is not as well attuned to contemplation as it might be. For this reason it is well for a person to do what is in his power to keep the body in a healthy condition, not so much in the way of animal strength as in the way of a well-balanced functioning of all his vital organs and of his nervous system. The exercises of *hatha yoga* are an excellent means towards this.

Sometimes people speak of feeling a pressure in the head, around the forehead, during meditation. This may be due to tension caused by trying too hard and this generates a certain anxiety which impedes the contemplation. In beginning to contemplate one should be very relaxed. It is not a matter of doing something but of letting it come. I once said to a person who I thought was rather tense, "Next time do not try to meditate at all, spend the time relaxing, especially your mind". She did so and said she had had a very good meditation without even trying. What made it a meditation, of course, was that she had the intention of being with God. This head-pressure may also be due simply to the fact that one is using one's brain in an unaccustomed way, intuitively instead of rationally. In this case the pressure wears off after a little while.

Another effect sometimes produced in the body by contemplation is a feeling of warmth, especially around the region of the heart. This is recognized as love, not an emotional but a spiritual love, calm and deep. Sometimes it can become quite intense and penetratingly painful and at the same time exquisitely sweet. This is what is called the fire of love. There is no problem here as to how to react to it because the heart is firmly set on God.

24

Temptations

By temptation I mean anything that attracts us away from God. Almost anything can be an occasion for this: reading, watching television, conversation, especially when accompanied by drinking, going to shows and parties. Obviously we cannot avoid all these things; we should have to go out of this world entirely. It is not so much the things themselves that tempt us as our disorderly reactions to them. Our inner disorder is the real source of our temptations and it is summed up in what are known as the seven deadly sins: pride, covetousness, lust, anger, gluttony, envy and sloth. These are not only sins in themselves but they represent tendencies which lead to many other sins.

Temptation implies a struggle between our desire and our will; we find ourselves wanting what our will does not approve of. It is a mistake to enter into dialogue with our desire, trying to work out how far we could safely give in to it. We are not impartial judges and we cannot trust our own thinking. The correct thing is to turn to God, but even then we must be careful not to talk to him too much about the temptation because we should find ourselves thinking about the temptation instead of praying. We should turn to God and forget the temptation, or at least keep our attention focused on God instead of on the temptation even though the temptation might be pressing in on our feelings all the time.

Some people think they have sinned merely because sinful thoughts come to their minds. We have no direct control over what comes to our minds. The most we can do is avoid certain things which are likely to cause us temptation, insofar as it may be possible to do so. When sinful thoughts come to mind and we feel we want them, even then there is no sin. We only sin when we deliberately surrender to them in our mind, even though we do not act on them externally. To act on them externally usually makes the sin worse because it is likely to have a bad effect on other people. It is important to build up a basic resistance to temptation by developing an interest in the spiritual life and especially by the practice of contemplation.

Temptation is due not only to our own evil inclinations; it can also come from the direct action of the evil spirit, whom we call Satan or the devil. The devil is a real person, of mighty intelligence and utterly committed to evil, and he is bent on bringing us to ruin. Fortunately for us his power is greatly curbed by God, but God allows him to tempt us to a certain extent, because if we struggle against the temptation and are victorious by the help of God, the result is our greater spiritual development and union with God.

As a clever boxer looks for points of weakness in his opponent and exploits them, so does the devil tempt us where we are weakest, but he also tempts people even when he sees no hope of making them sin. He does this to express his own rage at their holiness and to make them suffer. He certainly makes them suffer, because a person who is close to God suffers intensely when confronted with pressing suggestions of evil. St Catherine of Siena once experienced revolting temptations against chastity which greatly distressed her. When they were over she turned to Jesus and said, "Where were you, Lord, during all that time?" And he answered, "I was deep in your heart".

The temptations which Jesus himself suffered when on earth were of this kind. There could be no disorderly desires within his soul, no interior struggle between good and evil. His human nature was in perfect harmony with his godhead. But when evil suggestions were pressed on him by the devil and he felt the closeness of evil, the effect ot this on his own absolute purity of spirit was to cause the most intense suffering.

Some temptations are not aimed at immediate sin but rather at hindering spiritual good. Satan knows that in this way he will eventually bring about greater evil. That is why he does all he can to prevent a person from meditating. Through contemplative meditation a power of divine energy is poured into the world, an energy of love that captivates human hearts and draws them towards God. Therefore the devil does all he can to prevent this happening. Sometimes he gives people a repugnance to meditation; they would rather do anything than sit quietly to meditate. He gives them good works to do, making them feel they are serving

God in their neighbour; but his real purpose is to prevent them from meditating. We need to remember what St John of the Cross said: that one act of pure love gives more glory to God and is of more service to the Church than all other works together, presuming, of course, that these good works are not done out of pure love. And that is exactly what contemplative meditation is: pure love for God and for people. And this love is not idle in the life of a contemplative. It places him under the guidance of God to do the work that God wants to do. Because it is God's work it bears lasting fruit.

We should avoid temptations as much as possible, remembering our spiritual weakness and tendency to sin. We cannot expect God's help if we expose ourselves unnecessarily to the danger of sinning, but when we are doing God's work we must not be afraid of the temptations we encounter.

Spiritual growth comes through the struggle against temptation. When temptation cannot be avoided we should bear it peacefully, clinging to God and willing to suffer it as long as he wills. Left to ourselves we naturally like to serve God in the ways in which we feel strong and capable and we tend to ignore those areas in our personality where we are weak. But temptation touches us on our weak spots. In our efforts to resist the temptation we develop those weaker areas and make them strong, thus acquiring a well-balanced spiritual state. Furthermore, because we have to cling to God in time of temptation, we intensify the contact of our will with him, thereby giving him greater power over our lives.

25

Dark Night of The Soul

When a person first enters seriously on a spiritual life he usually experiences great enthusiasm for it. This is more than the natural enthusiasm one might feel on taking up a new and interesting occupation. God himself gives such a person a taste of his goodness and love and makes him feel that in comparison with the spiritual life all other pleasures are of no worth.

This state is known as first fervour and can come about in various ways. A person who has been reared from childhood to believe and practise the Christian faith may for many years take it very much for granted, looking on it as a duty that has to be fulfilled. But when some experience comes his way, perhaps quite trivial in itself, a new light is thrown on his faith and he begins to see how real and how wonderful it is. Or it may be that he discovers faith in God for the first time and faith in his Church, and from that moment on the world seems a different place. The charismatic movement, too, has had a similar effect in some people's lives. A religion that has hitherto meant little to them has suddenly come alive. There are others whose first approach to the spiritual life is through contemplative meditation. This is true although many people think that contemplative meditation is not for beginners. From the beginning God often gives such people remarkable signs of his love, making them aware of his presence.

Whatever may be the occasion of this spiritual awakening, the basic elements of it are usually the same: great joy and fervour in spiritual things and a strong desire to direct one's daily life towards God. In fact, the real value of this state of first fervour is that it does enable a person to bring about changes in his way of life, to give up whatever would be displeasing to God and to make time for spiritual reading and meditation. But this enthusiastic state usually does not last very long, perhaps a year or two; there is no fixed rule. God has different ways of dealing with every individual, but sooner or later a time comes when the enthusiasm fades away, meditation becomes difficult and boring and spiritual things on the whole lose their attraction. This can cause a person great distress, especially if he has a firm desire to get close to God. He thought he had been doing well and that with practice things would keep improving; then either suddenly or gradually everything goes wrong and, no matter what he does, he cannot recapture his feelings of devotion.

At this point it is very easy for a person to give up. If someone is cultivating a natural skill such as learning to play a musical instrument, he knows that his playing will improve with practice and that any time he takes up the instrument he will be ble to play it. Imagine, then, his amazement if one day he takes up the instrument and is simply unable to play it; although he continues to try day after day the result is always the same. Obviously he would decide that whatever the cause of his failure the only sensible thing to do would be to give up the effort. And this is what a person is likely to do when he finds that he cannot meditate anymore.

What he needs to know is that mediation is different from any natural skill. It is a gift from God, and our personal effort is only secondary. God gives joy and fervour in the beginning just as a little foretaste of what he has in store, to make a person realize how very worthwhile the spiritual life is, and to make it easy for them to give spiritual things a proper place in their lives. But if he continued to give them this joy and fervour they would begin to think of it as something belonging to themselves, something gained by their own efforts. They would become proud of it; and, instead of leading them to God, it would lead them away from him. God has to teach them to meditate as a service of love to him and not for their own satisfaction. It is for this reason, too, that God takes away our first fervour, so that we shall continue to meditate not for our own satisfaction but for love of him. Once a person realizes this he can settle down to the empty state with peace and contentment.

A priest engaged in the charismatic movement told me that

when a group develops over a period of about two years the first enthusiasm and fervour tend to fade away and they begin to feel they have come to a dead-end. Unless they know there is such a thing as contemplative meditation they are likely to give up entirely. In fact it has been said that contemplative meditation is a development and completion of charismatic prayer. Although the element of first fervour can indeed exist in contemplative meditation, real contemplative meditation usually has its beginning when the first fervour is over.

This state of spiritual dryness and emptiness is called by St John of the Cross the dark night of the soul, or more in particular the dark night of sense, because at a later stage there is what he calls the dark night of spirit. It is simply the transition from sense-satisfaction in meditation to a level that is more spiritual. If a person understands the meaning of this new dimension and adapts to it, the transition can be made with peace and contentment leading quickly to a deeper fulfilment.

When the time of first fervour has passed and the meditator has adjusted to the emptiness, boredom, and struggle with distractions that follow it, there then begins a long period of more truly spiritual development. Contemplation is then like a seed buried in the silence of this emptiness and which gradually develops, provided a person perseveres in the practice of meditation, until it envelops the soul in spiritual light and love.

This is the period during which a person is being healed of his inner disorders at a progressively deeper level and being formed in all Christlike virtues in the way I have described when speaking about virtue. It is the period which usually takes in the greater portion of a person's life. Throughout this time the inflowing of God's light and love keeps getting stronger, sometimes filling the soul with delight, sometimes blinding it with excessive light. In this latter state the soul experiences what is called the dark night of the spirit. It is a darkness caused by the excessive brightness of the divine inflowing. It brings the soul to a state of complete helplessness as regards all things spiritual. Meditation of any kind becomes quite impossible, and the light that blinds it shows up its hidden faults in a way that horrifies it. As someone said to me, "I am afraid to go out on the street because I feel that people would see how horrible I am". Yet at the same time deep down in its centre the soul is at peace and it knows that it is being held by God.

Apart from the great saints this dark night of the spirit is experienced by few people and then only for a short periods at a time, perhaps two or three months. Then the Lord gives them spiritual refreshment again. When eventually it has done its work the soul is completely purified and attains to union with God according to the measure of its capacity.

For although all people are called to holiness, that is, to be filled with divine life to the fullest measure of their capacity to receive it, they do not all have the same capacity. God has made great souls and little souls and a vast variety in between, but all are called to be perfect in their own measure and for them that is holiness. It is right that we should be inspired by the great saints but we should not compare ourselves with them or think that we must suffer the things that they suffered. We simply accept our life as it is, keep close to God in prayer, and he will lead us to that holiness that he has destined for us.

26

A Goal in Life

Life would be meaningless without a purpose. Consciously to do something without any purpose would be a form of insanity. We need to find a purpose for everything we do, but the immediate practical purposes that govern our daily lives are not adequate to give a purpose to life as a whole. That is why people take up so many projects and become disillusioned with them, because these are unable to give them the fulfilment that they seek. A certain wealthy man spent his money trying to find fulfilment in various ways, including the purchase of an expensive yacht and an aeroplane. Each new thing absorbed his enthusiasm for a while and then he got tired of it. Speaking of his areoplane, which he piloted himself, "There is nothing in it! I get into the plane, I go up in the air, I fly around, I come down again, I get out of the plane. There is nothing in it!"

Short-term purposes may satisfy us for a time but then they fail us and we look for more. Other purposes are long-term and may hold us for many years, but eventually they, too, are unsatisfying. The ambition to get to the top in one's business or to achieve fame in any of the ways in which this might happen, as a writer, a politician, a pop-singer, or many other ways, all this may keep a person going for quite a long time, but unless it is accompanied by a deeper spiritual fulfilment it will not bring happiness.

The simple fact is that the purpose of life is not to be found on earth. It lies beyond the grave, in the life that begins when this earthly life is over. Intellectual enquiry, scientific research cannot reveal this purpose to us. We can only get to know it by faith.

Faith is a word that sounds bad to many ears. It suggests trying to make ourselves believe something that we are not really sure of, as when we say, "I believe Mr Jones died in an accident but I am not quite sure". Faith means believing what someone tells us because we know that he is absolutely truthful and that he knows what he is talking about. Divine faith means that we believe what God tells us, only we have to be sure that it is really God who is telling us. It can be proved historically that a man lived on earth nearly two thousand years ago called Jesus Christ, who by his manner of life, his sublime teaching and the amazing miracles he worked made it clear that he was sent by God, in fact that he was God himself in human form. Jesus Christ formed a group of men into an organization known as his Church and told them to continue his teaching until the end of time and that he would be with them so that hostile forces would never overcome them.

Although all this can be proved historically it is not enough to convince a person's mind. Something else is needed, namely, a divine light given to the soul which makes it absolutely certain of the truth of this teaching. This is what we call the gift of faith. We Roman Catholics believe that the complete teaching of Christ subsists in our Church, that other Christian denominations have it in varying degrees, some having almost all of it, others much less. We believe that the gift of faith is given also to those who do not believe in Christ, provided that they avoid evil and do good. Essentially faith means that God makes himself known to a person and asks that person to dedicate his life to God in loving service. We know from the Bible that God wishes all humankind to be saved, and also that without faith it is impossible to please God. Therefore God must offer the gift of faith to everyone.

One quality of faith is that it gives certainty; certainty that God exists and that we have an obligation to serve him. One might wonder how can it be that people belonging to different religions can have different beliefs, even contradictory ones, and yet be equally certain that their beliefs are true. However, the fact is that wherever there is true faith, there is always the acceptance of a personal God and of our obligation to serve him. The contradictions arise from the workings of the human mind building-up religious doctrines that have not been revealed by God.

All true faith gives a purpose to life but the Christian faith presents this purpose very clearly. It shows us that God has a kingdom which is not of this world and that he has given us our span of earthly life to prepare ourselves with his help for our place in this kingdom. This we do by keeping close to God in prayer and by obedience to his will. In so doing, his divine life develops within us. It can truly be said that the purpose of life on earth is to develop God's life within us, or in other words, to live a supernatural life. What exactly do we mean by supernatural life? This needs some explanation.

If God had created us as human beings without inviting us to share his own life, then our happiness would consist in developing our human powers to the utmost, especially the power of contemplation, so that we could enjoy God shining through his creation. We should not see God as he is in himself, but we should be able to penetrate the inner beauty of creation and experience the love of God that fills it in a way that is impossible for us in our present sinful state. This happiness could be achieved by our own unaided efforts. It would be a human happiness; the proper and satisfying reward of a well-lived human life. But God decided not to leave us on a merely human level of existence. He decided to invite us to share his own life and to enjoy his own happiness. To make this possible he enriched our soul with a certain divine quality which we call sanctifying grace, in order to enable us to live in a divine dimension, which after death would admit us to the enjoyment of God as he is in himself. This sanctifying grace comes with the gift of faith, implying sorrow for sin and a turning to God in love.

On a human level God would be seen in a remote, rather impersonal way, although this would be a blissful experience, carrying with it an awareness of great love, but even the love would have something remote and impersonal about it. It would be similar to the experience of certain non-Christian mystics who feel they are drawn into a blissful experience of oneness with the being of the universe and bathed in an all-pervading love; yet the whole thing is impersonal. Very different is the intimacy that develops through the living of supernatural life. This is a deep contact between two persons, God and the human spirit. Or more correctly, the human spirit is drawn into a sharing of that life that exists between the three persons of the Blessed Trinity, Father, Son and Holy Spirit. In non-Christian or cosmic contemplation there is a sense of losing one's identity by being absorbed into a great and wonderful totality, but in Christian contemplation there is a person-to-person love-relationship. It can truly be called an indwelling: God lives in me and I live in God, yet far from losing my identity or being overwhelmed by the majesty of God his closeness to me emphasizes my own distinct individuality and makes me more completely myself.

In natural contemplation we know God in an impersonal way as the loving force giving being to all creation; in supernatural contemplation we know him as a personal friend, even as the bridegroom of our souls. Natural contemplation can be achieved by those who are seeking ultimate reality but have not yet attained to the gift of faith. Once this gift has been received all contemplation is supernatural. We do not have a choice between natural and supernatural happiness; we must either enter into the personal life of God or lose him entirely.

The purpose of life, then, is to find God ever more deeply, to share his life on earth through faith and love and hope, and after death to enter into the enjoyment of his happiness in a way that will never end. For many people this movement towards God takes place through a corresponding harmonious development on the human level: a happy home life in childhood, a good education leading to being qualified for the kind of job that one is suited for; then a happy marriage leading into an old age gladdened by the love of one's children and grandchildren, or else the fulfilment arising from consecration to God in some form of religious life. We all like to see our earthly life developing smoothly throughout its normal course, and it is altogether right and in accordance with God's will that we should work towards this end. But when things go wrong through no fault of our own and still more of it does happen to be our own fault, we easily become depressed, discouraged and even give way to despair.

Yet the failure of our life from an earthly standpoint does not necessarily mean its failure in the sight of God. If we react to our sins by true repentance, and to our mistakes and misfortunes by humbly accepting their consequences, and in everything submitting ourselves to the will of God with the help of constant prayer, then, although our life may be a failure on the human level, it is a success in the sight of God, because everything has contributed to the development of divine life in our soul. We have grown nearer to God by keeping close to him in all our misfortunes, and it is this intimacy with God that we carry with us into heaven when all earthly troubles are at an end. A successful life is a life that wins for us the happiness of heaven, and heavenly happiness is more easily gained by bearing suffering for love of God, than by enjoying the delights of earthly success.

27

Three Stages of Life

Life on earth can be divided into three stages, youth, middle-age and old age; childhood being regarded more as a preparation for life. A certain element of crisis usually marks the entry into each of these stages, and it depends on how a person reacts in such a crisis whether he will experience peace and fulfilment in the stage that follows.

First, there is the crisis of youth, when a child begins to discover himself as a person and to become aware of his freedom. There is the desire to rebel against authority and structures and at the same time an uncertainty as to how to cope with life. In one way this is an exciting challenge and yet not without an element of fear. Happy the young people who have learnt to meditate because the light they receive through it will guide them in their choices. It will lead them to seek advice from various people and to weigh their advice in the light that comes through meditation. They will know how to be true to their own inner being where God speaks to their heart, and will not let themselves be carried away by the opinions of other people who often speak according to their personal prejudices, and with little true understanding. Young people desire to assert their individuality, to do what they want to do and not to have things imposed on them by other people. The trouble is that they are as yet immature and likely to make mistakes when they trust their own insights. Meditation enables them to receive advice from other people, to absorb what is sound and practical in such advice, and yet to be true to their own deepest convictions in making their decisions.

Youth is a time of growing and becoming, of working to become qualified for certain jobs, of travelling to various parts of the world to see how other people live, of being on the look-out for a suitable partner with whom eventually to settle down to married life. There is a considerable amount of idealism in this process of opening out on life, and those are fortunate for whom this idealism becomes even to a moderate extent a reality. In many cases there is disillusionment when hopes are disappointed and life settles down into a rather dull and dreary monotony. This is the crisis that often comes in the early yars of middle life, when youthful ambition fails to achieve the goals it had set itself and life does not seem to offer much that is really worth living for. And even when a person does achieve his goals they do not seem to be all that they promised to be and they leave him unsatisfied. One is reminded of the story of the cabin-boy, who by hard work and study worked his way up through the ranks until at the age of forty-five he became admiral of the navy. Then he sat down and wept because, "Now," he said, "I have to be an admiral all my life".

What is needed in order to cope with the crisis of middle age is to change one's attitude towards life. It is like changing gear in a car; you use one gear going up a hill and another gear on the level road. If youth is a time of growing and becoming middle age is a time of being and giving. Youth is a time of drawing things to oneself in the way of knowledge and experience; middle age is a time of sharing with others what one has achieved. It matters little enough what a person's circumstances are; if he knows how to give himself to his work and to give himself to people with a generous and loving heart, he will find happiness in almost any circumstances. And it is by giving himself first and foremost to God that everything else falls into place. The middle years then become the golden period of life when a person makes his maximum contribution to society, and in many cases he himself continues to grow as a person. I heard of someone who compared Abraham Lincoln with many other men he had met at various times with spaces of a few years in between. He said these other men were just the same every time he met them but Lincoln had grown greater every time. That is what comes of knowing how to infuse an ideal of loving service into the ordinary activities of daily life.

This middle period of life is in fact a period that should extend well into old age. This would indeed happen if people knew how to make love the dominant inspiration of their lives and subjected their bodies to a wholesome discipline in matters of food, sleep and exercise. But eventually old age comes to everyone if life continues and with it a new crisis develops. As age and infirmity increase a person becomes unable to do many of the things he did so well before. He becomes more dependent on other people. He comes to feel that he is a burden on people and sometimes even that people do not want him. He may suffer from loneliness, isolation and neglect. All this is hard to bear, and such a person may seek consolation by living in the past, thinking of the happy times of long ago and eventually not thinking at all but living a kind of vegetable existence.

Here, also, the remedy lies in a change of attitude, in getting into a different mental gear. Instead of looking back, the thing is to look forward and work for the future. One might wonder what future such old people could look forward to. It is the entry into eternal life. Here faith is essential because only faith gives a satisfying purpose to life. For one who has faith the whole span of human life is a journeying towards the kingdom of God, our heavenly home for which we were made. And now one is getting near the end of the journey. It is a joy to look forward to journey's end, to meeting friends who have gone on before, and above all to meeting the God whom one has already learnt to love. It is good, then, that age and feebleness have left us with more time on our hands; it is good even when our friends are less inclined to spend time with us.

It is now more than ever that we reap the fruits of the meditation we have practised throughout our lives. The invisible world has become very real to us and we gladly bear the discomforts and inconveniences that age brings to us because we know we are on the threshold of a life where youth and freedom and love will be ours for ever. And whatever we have to suffer in our declining years we see it as a spiritual cleansing preparing our souls for the life to come. I have seen old people whose faces shone with the life of eternity. One who said, "I am like a ship riding at anchor in the bay, waiting for the signal to enter port". That was my father who died at seventy-four. My mother's last words to me were, "I am going to heaven to pray for you". She died at ninety-six. Any traveller who is looking forward to a happy homecomeing will be glad to know he is coming near the end of a long and wearisome journey. It is this expectancy of everlasting life to come that gives joy to the declining years of our life on earth.

28

Perseverance

People find so many reasons for not persevering in the various projects they undertake that the idea of perseverance as an ideal to be aimed at comes to have little or no meaning for them. People are constantly changing their jobs and for quite good reasons: more money, shorter hours, more interesting work. On the other hand they will sometimes force themselves to presevere in doing jobs that have become too difficult for them: the money is good, they have good friends on the job, and they do not want to admit that they are unhappy in their work. So they keep going and eventually get a breakdown. Then they have to give up their job and it takes them months to recover. So on the whole the idea of perseverance or permanent commitment is not looked upon as something desirable.

    This is true with regard to the examples I have just given, but there are cases in which perseverance is important. One is in the matter of vocation. By vocation I mean a divinely implanted capacity and inclination for some particular way of life. One man may feel that he can never be happy unless he is pilot of an aeroplane, another is only happy when surrounded by pots of paint. There are many men and women who have within themselves a deep desire for some particular kind of occupation. The occupations in question can be of endless variety, but such persons can never be happy unless they are doing what they want to do. Not everyone has such a clear sense of vocation and there are many who can turn their hands to different kinds of jobs with equal ease. There are others, too, in whom the vocation lies deep in the unconscious mind and they are not aware of it and they waste much time trying various things because they do not know what they really want. Their minds get obscured by the requirements of a civilization that is geared towards science and technology and fails to satisfy the spiritual aspirations of the human personality.

What a person needs is to look into his heart and ask himself what does he really want. Some people are afraid to do this because they think, "It is not what I want that is important but what God wants". But vocation consists precisely in that God puts into people an instinct for what he wants them to do. If they look into their true selves they will discover his will. But we must beware of our disordered selves, that selfishness in us that seeks our immediate satisfaction instead of our true good. It is here that meditation gives us light to discern the true from the false. Unfortunately circumstances often make it impossible for a person to follow his true vocation and he has to settle for a second best.

As soon as a person has found his vocation, whether it be the ideal or the best that can be had under the circumstances, then he should make up his mind to stay with it as long as he lives. I do not mean always doing the same job but always following the same way of life. If you pull out of a thing when the going is difficult you have failed to stand up to a challenge and you have missed an opportunity for personality growth. We like to keep developing our strong points. This tends to make us unbalanced, for in difficulties it is often our weak points that are touched upon and these are developed by being called into action thus giving us a balanced development of personality. Even when a person has to settle for a way of life that he does not really want, if he faces up to it and gives it his best, it will develop qualities in him that will prepare him for what may turn out to be his real life-work at a later date, and he would not have been ready for this had it come to him at an earlier stage. People are inclined to think they are missing something if they do not try their hand at many different things. This is all right while searching for one's vocation, but when one has found one's vocation the only right thing is to stay with it and grow to one's full stature by means of it. To do otherwise would be like planting a shrub and rooting it up every few weeks in the hope of putting it into better soil. Such action would only kill it. Choose favourable soil before planting but then leave it there and let it grow. Or, as the saying is "Bloom where you are planted".

Another case where perseverance is important and even vitally necessary is in the spiritual life. The whole purpose of our life on earth is to grow towards God. Having the right vocation in life is important for our earthly happiness and development but to persevere in the spiritual life is important for our eternal destiny. By spiritual life I do not mean giving God that minimum of service that is necessary to secure our eternal salvation, but rather devoting ourselves whole-heartedly to the development of the divine life within us. The only thing we can take with us into eternity is this sharing in God's life which we have developed on earth in the obscurity of faith. After death it will be as though a veil will be drawn aside and we shall enjoy that very life of God which we developed on earth without seeing it. The more we developed that life on earth the more we shall possess of it in heaven. St Teresa of Avila tells us that to attain one additional degree of glory in heaven would be worth a lifetime of suffering on earth. Therefore, even granted that we were sure of attaining to the vision of God in heaven, there is nothing so much worth working for on earth as an increase of this heavenly happiness. But in fact we cannot be sure of getting to heaven and the only safe thing is to work for it with all our strength. However, the most important reason of all for persevering in our spiritual life is that God has a right to our absolute and unrestricted love and service. And yet unfortunately there are many who do not persevere.

The reasons for this are very varied but there are some things that stand out more frequently as explaining why people give up. Sin, of course, in a obvious cause. A person cannot be offending God and drawing close to him at the same time. It is different when a person is in the habit of committing sin and is trying to overcome it but is not able to do so immediately. Such a person is really getting closer to God in spite of his lapses into sin which he repents of each time. But for the person who sins and does not repent there can be no spiritual life. Even an occasional serious sin, sincerely repented of, does not greatly injure one's spiritual life, but a general carelessness about so-called "small" sins is far more dangerous because it renders a person insensitive to the guidance of God and less inclined to repent even of serious sins. If you throw a ball to the ground it hops up again; if you roll it down a slope it remains at the bottom. The occasional serious sin in a person who is seeking God is usually followed by repentance and this is often so sincere that it leaves the sinner closer to God than before, but gradual carelessness about smaller sins leads to carelessness about greater sins, until a person begins to live in sin without any desire for repentance.

Another reason why people give up the spiritual life is that they become too interested in other things. It is right to be interested in everything that goes to make up our daily life insofar as these things are God's will for us, but we must keep our priorities in proper order and not allow ourselves to cling to anything in a selfish way.

It is easy to take up some hobby or work which gradually develops in such a way that there is no time left for meditation. We do not want to give up our meditation. We do our best to fit it in. For a while we force ourselves to do it early in the morning or late at night, but this does not work as we need our sleep, and so meditation goes. We never think of giving up the work that consumes our time or of reducing it to more moderate proportions; or if such thoughts come to us we quickly put them away as being out of the question. And so meditation disappears.

Early this century Monsignor Robert Hugh Benson wrote a book entitled *An Average Man*. It was the story of a young man who on hearing a sermon got the grace of a sudden conversion to the Catholic Church. He immediately went to see a priest and began a course of instructions. All went well until, about half way through the course, a relative of his died and left him an estate in the country. All the enthusiasm that he had about becoming a Catholic now got transferred to looking after his estate. At first he would write to apologize for missing an instruction. Then he would miss another and another and he would be ashamed to apologize any more. Eventually he forgot about becoming a Catholic. In giving this book the title *An Average Man* Monsignor Benson evidently knew that defections of this kind were by no means a rare occurrence.

There are others who give up the spiritual life for no obvious reason except that they get tired of it. This will not happen if a person has been faithful to grace, if he has listened to the guidance that comes through meditation and tries to follow it. But it is so easy not to listen, to ignore the voice of the Lord when he speaks in our conscience to tell us what he wants. Then gradually the inflowing of God becomes weaker, the spiritual life comes to have less meaning for us and eventually we give it up altogether. I was once visiting an enclosed monastery and I remarked to the monk who was showing me around that it must be very easy to become holy in such a way of life. "We certainly have every opportunity," he said, "but it is surprising how one can give up". He was not referring to a monk leaving the monastery, but to a monk who while living on in the monastery and observing all the rules externally, had yet given up all desire of living a spiritual life. One might wonder why such a person would not leave the monastery, yet if he had spent many years there and had got accustomed to the way of life and was not qualified to earn his living in the world, it is understandable that he might choose to stay where he was.

But it is alarming to think that one could dwell in an ideal atmosphere for developing union with God and yet have no desire for it.

There is a parable in the gospel that well illustrates the reasons why people give up the spiritual life. It is the parable of the sower. (Matthew 13:1-23.) A sower went out to sow his seed and it fell on different kinds of soil which had different effects on its growth. The seed is the Word of God and it can be considered here as applying to the first time a person hears about contemplative meditation. Some seed falls by the wayside and the birds devour it before it has a chance to grow. That means that when a person hears about meditation the devil immediately suggests a reason for not doing it, such as: you have no time; you have not the right temperament; it is dangerous to go so deep into spiritual things. People who listen to such promptings do not even begin. Other seed fell on rocky ground where there was but little soil. It sprung up quickly but when drought came it withered because its roots were not deep. This refers to the people who are enthusiastic when they hear about meditation, but later on when they meet with criticism and ridicule from their friends on account of it they give up because they have not acquired a deep conviction as to its worth. Again other seed falls among thorn bushes; it takes root deeply enough but so do the thorn bushes that surround it and these grow up and choke it. This refers to those people who take a deep and serious interest in meditation but they are also interested in other things. The cares and problems of life and the various enterprises in which they are engaged so occupy their mind and take up their time that eventually they have no time left for meditation. Finally there is the seed that falls on good ground and bears fruit. This refers to the people who continue to meditate until the end of their lives. Yet even here there is a difference: some bear fruit a hundredfold, some sixtyfold and some only thirtyfold.

So even among those who keep up the practice of meditation not all do it with the same whole-heartedness. It is the privilege of our freedom to decide how much we want to give to God. There are some who reject him altogether, usually not directly but because there are other things they want more. And of those who give themselves to his service there are many who keep back a certain amount for themselves. Yet even if they do so, it is still a great thing that they seek God and that they persevere to the end.

A question that naturally comes to mind is, what can a person do in order to be sure of persevering? And the simple answer is that there is no way of being sure. As long as we live on earth there is the possibility of turning away from God, but it can truly be said that the closer we get to him the less likely are we to turn away.

There are certain ways in which we can help to secure our perseverance. We should have a clear idea as to the purpose of our life on earth, which is to serve God faithfully so as to enter the kingdom of heaven when we die and share his happiness for ever. We should realize that this involves a struggle and that to fail in this struggle means to lose God for ever and to suffer the everlasting pains of hell. God is good but sin is terrible, and not even God can save us if we freely cling to sin. To be aware that there is danger makes us all the more careful to avoid it. Our human frailty is such that if we think we are going to go to heaven in any case we can easily relax our efforts and drift away from God and so lose him. Our Lord gave us a stern warning when he said, "The gate is narrow and the way is hard, that leads to life, and those who find it are few". (Matthew 7:14) Thus, to see heaven as our goal, as a prize to be won by serious efforts and prayer, is a great means of securing our perseverance. But we must keep this thought before our minds frequently. We must never forget where we are going. If a traveller forgets where he is going he easily loses his way.

Another way in which we can help to secure our perseverance is by not feeling sure of ourselves. We are taught that self-confidence is a desirable quality, but the confidence of a Christian is rooted not in himself but in God. Since perseverance, like all virtue, is a gift from God, the person who feels sure of himself is the very one who is likely to defect. But the person who knows his weakness and turns to God for help is the one who will persevere. When Jesus told his disciples that they would all desert him in his passion Peter was indignant and said that even though the others deserted him he never would. Yet he was the one who denied him that very night and swore that he never knew him. Had Peter not been seen so sure of himself and had he said, "Lord, I know how weak I am, please help me to be faithful to you", things would have been very different.

When people fail a number of times they often get disheartened and give up. Yet the truth is that perseverance consists in always beginning again. Struggle is never a continual series of victories. It consists in often falling and rising again. In fact a number of failures can add up to a great victory. This happens when a person picks himself up after each fall and begins again with renewed energy. Each time there is the lesson of experience, a greater distrust of one's weakness, a more whole-hearted turning to the power of God, until eventually a person rises to fall no more. The whole philosophy of perseverance can be summed up in one word: the only failure is to stop trying.

29

The Sacred Humanity of Christ in Contemplative Meditation

Contemplative meditation, also referred to as contemplation or mystical prayer, is characterized by an emptying of the mind of all thoughts and images and an attentiveness of the heart which can sometimes develop into deep absorption. This can create a problem for Christians who know that we cannot go to God except through Jesus Christ as man. Jesus said, "No one comes to the Father, but by me." (John 14:6) Are we then turning away from Jesus when we enter into this contemplation that is without thought or image?

We must bear in mind that mystical contemplation can be of two kinds: natural and supernatural. Both are mystical because in neither are we making use of our thinking mind but rather are we allowing our mind to enter an intuitive state where it is entirely passive and receptive.

This intuitive state can be brought about by our own efforts, by using suitable techniques to make our mind a blank, and we thus open ourselves to an inflowing from the Ground of Being, that Absolute Being which underlies and penetrates and transcends all particular kinds of being. It is God, in fact, but contacted only as the source of creation and not as revealing himself in a personal way. This contact in its early stages beings a feeling of calmness and peace. As it develops it brings a sense of God's presence and love and very deep joy, yet there is always something impersonal about it. It is like being aware of great love and not knowing who loves you. An agnostic once had this experience and she said, "I feel great love; I am afraid to call it God".

This is natural contemplation, and it can be considered the highest accomplishment of our human nature by its own powers. But in itself it is not sufficient for salvation. It can exist in a person who has no faith, although God may very well offer the gift of faith at such times by revealing himself in a personal way and asking the person to surrender to his will. If that lady who had experienced great love in her contemplation had said, "Lord, it is you; I want to belong to you," she would have received the gift of faith and her contemplation would have become supernatural. God wants everyone to be saved. Therefore he must offer faith to everyone because without faith it is impossible to please God. This faith comes through Jesus Christ even though such a person might not know this.

A Christian has been incorporated into the Mystical Body of Christ by Baptism, and provided he is in a state of grace, all the good actions he does with a good intention and in suitable circumstances have a supernatural value. This is true of actions which in themselves are neither morally good or bad, such as playing the piano or having a glass of beer or a game of golf. Natural contemplation is in the same category as these. It is the highest accomplishment of human nature. If engaged in at a time when it does not interfere with any duty, it has a supernatural value; but it is not supernatural contemplation. It would be something similar to playing classical music, reading poetry, appreciating the excellence of art or architecture. It is on the same level as these, yet more excellent.

A Christian can practise this natural contemplation by deliberately trying to make his mind a blank in order to make contact with the Ground of Being. In itself it is an excellent occupation, bringing relaxation and peace of mind and even deep happiness. But it is not Christian contemplation. It does little to being about an increase of divine life in the soul, and it may even turn a person away from God by making him proud of his achievement, or by toppling over into gross sensuality, as sometimes happens with highly artistic temperaments. It would seem to be this natural contemplation that St Teresa of Avila suspected at times in her sisters when they spent a lot of time in a state of absorption; she would encourage them to come out of it and pray for the Church or do some active work or take some fresh air. Even in her own case at one period, submitting to advice she received, she tried to exclude all thoughts from her mind, and although she felt a deep joy of God's presence, she regretted this afterwards as not being the right kind of contemplation.

How, then, is a Christian to be sure that he is not practising natural contemplation but genuine Christian contemplation which is supernatural? It is by recognizing that natural contemplation is due to our own efforts but supernatural contemplation is due to God's initiative. Supernatural contemplation introduces us into a personal love-relationship with our heavenly Father through Jesus Christ in the power of his Holy Spirit. In doing so it reproduces in our souls the sentiments that filled the heart of Christ when he was on earth, sentiments that concerned his work of redemption and that now enable us to become sharers with him in his work. All Christian contemplation is redemptive.

But the question remains: how in practice do we enter upon this supernatural contemplation? And the answer is: by turning to Jesus Christ so that by the power of his Spirit working within us we may be united with our heavenly Father. To do this we must not make hard and fast rules about how we should pray. We should desire to be led by the Holy Spirit and then allow ourselves to pray whatever way we feel inclined. We should allow our prayer to change even from moment to moment as the Spirit leads us and without making any deliberate decisions about it. If we contemplate by our own efforts, it is natural; if we allow God to do it in us, it is supernatural. And until God draws us into contemplation we must pray by actively using our minds and not by trying to "make our minds a blank". In the early stages God draws us into contemplation, not by any powerful intervention but merely by giving us a gentle inclination to be quiet. We must be careful not to ignore this inclination by persisting in the active use of our minds.

There are many states in which a person may find himself during prayer, and these states can sometimes change easily from one to another, as it were backwards and forwards, and I am not referring to the higher states of mystical prayer.

A person will often begin by looking at Jesus Christ in some scene of his life, listening to his words and speaking to him, then quietly remaining in his presence in a simple attitude of love. This is discursive mediation merging into the prayer of simplicity. Then it frequently happens that one is drawn away into emptiness of all thought. It is the Spirit of Jesus within him who is drawing him into the deep centre of his soul, there to work within him those delicate anointings of love, of which St John of the Cross speaks. Far from turning away from the sacred humanity, he is more deeply immersed in it. He is united with Jesus, no longer at the more superficial level of conscious thought and imagination but at the deeper, unconscious level of the spirit. It requires considerable self-surrender to let go one's thinking mind and be at rest in this state.

While in this contemplative state, the Spirit of Christ will sometimes activate a person's mind silently to pour out words of praise or sorrow for sin, or to keep company with Jesus in his passion with a vivid use of the imagination, or in other ways to converse with him in words of love. But this is not discursive meditation. It is not initiated by the person who is praying but by the Spirit of God dwelling within him and therefore it is part of contemplation. Some of the effusions of love expressed by St Teresa in her writings evidently came from a heart deeply immersed in contemplation.

Whether contemplation takes place only in the deep, unconscious regions of the spirit or expresses itself in divinely-inspired meditations and colloquies, it is producing a most important effect in the soul. This consists in bringing about a spiritual transformation by eliminating faults and implanting virtues, but particularly by reproducing in the soul the dispositions of Christ. Christ begins to give the soul a share in the feelings which he himself had when on earth: his love for his Father, his prayer to his Father, his affliction of heart on account of sin, his spirit of self-immolation, his love for the whole human race and his longing to save them from hell. These attitudes of his heart he communicates to the souls of his contemplatives according to the special vocation and capacity of each. In fact it is Christ himself who lives again his sacrificial life in such souls: he prays to his Father in them, he suffers in them, he looks out on the world through their eyes, and through them he draws hearts to himself. People look at such contemplatives. It is Christ they see in them and to Christ they are drawn, or else they reject and persecute them as they reject and persecuted Christ.

It is often thought that a person needs to spend a considerable time getting to know Jesus Christ through reading and discursive meditation before he becomes capable of contemplation. But this is not true. We all have an intuitive power in our mind as well as a thinking power, and God can claim the attention of this intuitive power at any time provided we do not resist him. Many people experience supernatural contemplation without knowing it, and even many children.

There are quite a number of Christians who have but little knowledge of Jesus Christ and little desire to get to know him better. They are not inclined to pray to him; when they try, they do not know what to say. But they are attracted by silent meditation and by the use of techniques such as the *mantra* and the awareness of breathing. This meditation gives them peace of mind and gradually makes the spiritual world seem more real to them.

Being Christians they will find themselves using *mantras* invoking the name of Jesus. They will gradually come to realize that they know very little about him and they will want to start increasing their knowledge by reading and reflection. They began with contemplation and the contemplation made them realize their need to nourish their thinking minds with the knowledge of Jesus Christ. Perhaps in the beginning this contemplation was natural, but who can say at what point it becomes supernatural? It is only when a person has no faith and no desire for faith and does meditation only for the sake of its psychological advantages that we can be certain that his meditation is a purely natural activity. However, as a person makes progress in Christian contemplation he needs to be on his guard against lapsing into natural contemplation. But one needs to be quite clear about the following point: the state of being in a mental void, without thoughts or images, can be either natural and cosmic or supernatural and Christian, depending on whether we produce it ourselves to allow God to produce it in us. Even if it begins by being natural and then at some point we surrender ourselves to God in love, it becomes supernatural.

Therefore the attitude of a Christian in contemplation should be to surrender himself to a divine influence that will draw him into the heart of Christ, there to find intimacy with the holy Trinity.

30

Our Invisible Friends

There is a kind of meditation which can be called cosmic. It is based simply on the relationship between absolute and relative being, between the Creator and the creature, and takes no account of the human condition. Certain non-Christian forms of meditation are like this; they lead a person to the experience of the oneness of all things and of losing oneself in a great totality in which there is peace and love, yet an impersonal kind of love — one does not know where it is coming from. This is what we call natural mysticism, an experience of the all-pervading Being underlying all creation in other words, the immanence of God in his creation. It is entirely impersonal.

Christian mysticism, however, is quite different. (Incidentally, mysticism is just another word for contemplative meditation, though usually understood to refer to higher stages of it.) Christian mysticism is set in the human situation. It takes into account the history of salvation: the creation and fall of man, redemption through Christ and the continuation of Christ's saving work through the Church. It is entirely personal. It has to do with personal relationships between God and his people and with relationships among the people themselves. Natural mystics would say that this injures the pure transcendence of meditation, introducing into it historical facts and people.

On the contrary, Christian contemplation is more in accordance with our nature. It recognizes that we are matter as well as spirit, body as well as soul, and that we need visible and tangible things to help us into the spiritual and transcendent. And in any case we cannot pretent that we do not exist in a historical situation. Sin is a historical fact; redemption through Christ is a historical fact, and to mediate as if these facts did not exist would be to separate our meditation from spiritual realities that govern our life. And yet Christian contemplation is truly transcendent because it leads us into the world of supernatural realities in a way that surpasses the power of our thinking mind. And in this supernatural world we are surrounded by people who are intensely interested in our contemplation.

First of all there are the three persons of the godhead itself, the Blessed Trinity: Father, Son and Holy Spirit. The Father is eternally begetting his Son. Father and Son are eternally breathing forth their Spirit. All three are distinct and equal. All possess the same godhead; three persons in one God. This is the inner life of God; natural or cosmic contemplation knows nothing of it. But the Christian soul is drawn into this mysterious and intensely personal life of the godhead.

Then there are the angelic spirits, pure intelligences, real persons although without bodies, radiating goodness and beauty and love. Their joy is to contemplate God without ceasing, and it is also a joy to them to see us engaged in contemplation. We are doing in the darkness of faith what they are doing in the full light of vision and they know that we are preparing ourselves to share the happiness that they enjoy. They have power also to help us, particularly those angels that God has given us to be our guardians. Each particular human person has been given an angel guardian, who acts as an instrument of God's love in our regard, to protect us from evil whether of soul or body. While this angelic influence is always present, the extent to which we receive it depends very much on how receptive we are. Hence we should often think of our guardian angel as a companion who is always with us, so that we develop a friendly relationship towards him.

Apart from the angels we have many human friends in the invisible world, especially those whom we knew and loved while they lived on earth. Also the saints to whom we have a special devotion. They follow our spiritual progress with the greatest interest and love, helping us in many ways that we are not aware of.

Outstanding among all the saints and in a category all of her own is the Blessed Virgin Mary. She is the queen of heaven, next to God himself in power and glory. When she lived on earth she was an ordinary village girl in Nazareth, yet she had been chosen to be the mother of Jesus, and because Jesus is God as well as man she can truly be called the mother of God. To prepare her for this unique dignity she was preserved free from original sin, from that wound that sin has caused in our nature as a result of the sin committed by the first parents of our race. This is known as her Immaculate Conception. From the beginning of her life she was sinless and holy, with a holiness surpassing that of any of the saints. She united herself heart and soul with the great work of redemption that her Son Jesus had come to accomplish, standing with him by the cross on which he was dying, spiritually sacrificing her life along with his for the salvation of the world. Because she was so closely associated with Jesus in his great act of redemption she is equally associated with him in imparting the fruits of redemption. God wishes to honour her by giving us many graces through the power of her intercession. There is no one in heaven more interested in our meditation than she is, or better able to help us.

She has a special power of enlarging our hearts in meditation in order to receive God in greater depth. Centuries before the coming of Christ on earth God had been preparing the way for his coming by choosing a single nation, the Israelites, and developing among them a sense of their sinfulness, their need of redemption, and a longing for the coming of him who would save them from their sins. Unfortunately, in the nation as a whole this desire for a saviour became corrupt and thought of only in terms of political freedom. Yet there was within the nation a spiritual core of holy people who longed for a saviour who would free them from their sins. As the centuries passed, drawing closer to the time of Christ's birth, this longing became more and more intense. Desire enlarges one's capacity to receive, opening out within one's soul vast empty areas that call out to be filled. It was like a great prayer rising up from the soul of the nation calling upon God to send the saviour. All these desires of the centuries came to a head in the soul of the Blessed Virgin Mary. We can imagine her as she is often depicted in paintings, kneeling in prayer, asking God to send the promised saviour into the world. That prayer contained within itself the intensity of all the prayers that had ever been said for this intention and it surpassed them all. And it was to Mary's prayer and to the immaculate purity of her soul that the answer was given. An angel appeared to announce the event, and the second person of the Blessed Trinity took flesh in her womb.

So great was the attractive power of Mary's holiness and of her prayerful desire that it drew God down to her from heaven. That same attractive power of hers will draw God more powerfully into our souls in contemplation. As our spiritual mother she is always helping us and nothing pleases her so much as to increase in our hearts that longing for God which so wonderfully filled her own heart. Yet the more we consciously turn to her and recognize the love she has for us, the more powerfully shall we feel her influence. Of course in the actual state of contemplation we do not think of anything unless God inspires the thoughts, but it is often helpful at the beginning of our meditation to remind ourselves that we are not only entering into the presence of God but also into the company of Mary, the queen of heaven, and of a vast number of angels and saints. All of them have great joy in seeing us beginning in a dark and faltering way the occupation that is their eternal delight in heaven.

While we gladly think of the many invisible friends with whom contemplation puts us in contact, we must not overlook the fact that we have invisible enemies as well. These are the devils, fallen angels, who in their pride refused to submit to God, even though he was only asking their submission in order that he might share his happiness with them. They preferred to plunge themselves into hell instead. Because the angelic mind is so clear-sighted, when an angel makes a decision, it is final. He can see no reason for changing his mind because he saw all the reasons before he made his decision. Therefore there could be no redemption for the devils. They cannot repent and they do not want to. Their will is fixed against God. They are entirely committed to evil. Everything they do is evil, and they never give up. Since they cannot injure God directly they try to injure him by snatching us humans away from him.

Thus we live in danger of losing God, not only on account of our own sinful inclinations but also on account of the attacks we suffer from these evil spirits. They have a certain power to influence our imagination and our feelings, but they cannot touch our will directly. Our will is free. The devil is not always to blame for the evil thoughts and desires that come to us. They are mostly due to our own selfish inclinations. But when they come suddenly and with intensity and without any obvious cause and when our nature recoils against them, then they are the work of the devil. But of course the devil will often get in on our own disorderly feelings in order to make the temptation more severe.

Our soul is like a battlefield where good and evil spirits are fighting for possession. The evil spirits want to control us and lead us to sin. The good spirits, the angels, are fighting to save us and keep us in contact with God. What makes the outcome of the struggle so uncertain is our freedom of will. Our own spiritual power is very little in comparison with the forces of good and evil that are trying to influence us. We are like snowflakes tossed about in a storm. But we have the power to choose which side we are going to join — God and his holy angels, or else the devils. The devils are clever in deceiving us and making us think evil is good. So we need to keep very close to God in order to be guided by his truth and supported by his love. The angels are God's servants whom he uses to protect us.

Such then is the vast world of invisible beings in which we live and move and have our being. If we lose contact with God we are at the mercy of hostile forces. If we keep close to God, as we do in meditation, we are supported by him, and we also have the support and friendship of his angels and saints and especially of the great queen of heaven, the Blessed Virgin Mary.

31

The Best Way to Help People

There are many who think that meditation is a selfish occupation. To sit in a comfortable posture, relax your mind, let all your worries fade away and enter into a state of calm contentment and even bliss — surely that is just an escape from the realities of life and a blameworthy preoccupation with oneself. Even if it were such an escape it is better than many selfish and sinful things that people do in an effort to escape from the stresses of life. But it is not such an escape; it is a powerful means of understanding life's realities and entering into deep commitment towards the needs of the world around us.

Meditation gives spiritual enlightenment. It enables us to understand situations and what can be done to help. It also shows us how to mind our own business and not interfere where we are not needed. For meditation surrenders us to the guidance of God. God knows exactly what each person needs at every moment. He uses us humans as his instruments. He wants us to help one another but under his guidance.

Meditation opens us to God's guidance. If we are not guided by God in our activities, we shall often do the wrong things for people, giving in to our own impulses instead of doing what is needed. One person might be a gifted organizer, and as long as he is organizing something that seems good he does not stop to think whether God wants it or not. God might have other plans and better ones. Or God might want someone else to do this work.

Another person might have a gift of healing. He may think that God wants him to heal everyone, not realizing that God has his own times and ways for healing people; there are some disabilities God does not wish to heal but wishes them to be suffered with loving patience.

There are some who would prefer to regard themselves as collaborators with God rather than as his instruments, because the world collaborator gives more emphasis to human dignity. They overlook the fact that we have no independence in relation to God, and no initiative. Our most brilliant insights and ideas only come to our minds because God put them there, and if at any time we do our own thing rather than what God inspires, we are damaging his work rather than helping it. It is when we leave ourselves entirely at his disposal that our personal contribution is at its best. Because God is our Creator, the more there is of God in us the more perfectly we are ourselves. And yet there is something positive that we do contribute to God's work because each individual is a unique instrument in God's hands, doing his work in a way that is different from anyone else.

God has a work for everyone to do in life. We are all his children, part of the one great human family. He wants to draw us all to himself, into the everlasting happiness of his kingdom. He wants us to help one another towards this end. But we can help people towards God only to the extent that we ourselves are filled with the Spirit of God. We need contemplative meditation in order to be filled with his Spirit. We cannot give what we do not possess. Even the very material services that we might do for people could work to their harm unless we are guided by God in doing them. Prayer must be the soul of all good works if they are to be fruitful. What good is material welfare if it does not lead a soul to God? But while material good works need the vivifying power of contemplation, contemplation itself can stand alone.

There is a way of helping people which is purely spiritual. It is by uniting with Christ and drawing from him the graces that people need. This is what we do whenever we pray for people. We ask God to help them directly, and there are innumerable cases in which people believe that remarkable answers have been given to their prayers; in which God has given not only spiritual graces but even material good things in answer to someone else's prayers.

There are some favours that are more difficult to obtain from God because of the obstacles that exist in the persons for whom we pray. For example, when we pray that a person be converted to God from a life of sin, we are asking for something that requires a profound change within a person's heart, a change which perhaps he himself does not want to make. To obtain this requires more than just a few casual prayers. It requires the kind of prayer that is the result of deep desire and close union with the heart of Christ who died to save us from our sins. It may also require a willingness to suffer in union with the sufferings of Christ.

Contemplative meditation gives us this close union with Christ and enables us to draw from the fruits of his death by which he redeemed the world. While his death was sufficient to save us all, it does not save us without our co-operation. He wants us to join in with him not only to save ourselves but to help to save others as well. Through contemplative meditation we achieve this deep union with Christ that enables us to draw from him powerful blessings to help other people. What greater help could we give another person than to save him from hell and enable him to go to heaven?

There is a story told by Monsignor Robert Hugh Benson in his book *The Light Invisible*. It was told to him by an old priest who from time to time received visions of the invisible world. This priest went to visit a friend of his in a convent of enclosed nuns whose special vocation it was to pray for the conversion of sinners. The community were occupied when he arrived and he was asked to wait for a while in the chapel. The chapel was dark when he entered and at first he thought he was the only one there. But as his eyes became accustomed to the dim light he became aware of the figure of a nun kneeling before the tabernacle. He began to think about her and wonder why she had chosen such a life. There in the austere, dark chapel her life seemed so cold and loveless. He felt a wave of anger coming upon him. Surely this was no life for a woman. How much better had she shared the warmth and love of a happy home and brought joy to her husband and children. And then suddenly the scene changed. The chapel became alive with spiritual vibrations. In the tabernacle a great heart was beating in unison with the heart of the kneeling nun. Together they formed a kind of spiritual engine, like in a factory where two wheels are linked together by a belt and you cannot be sure which one is moving the other. And so from the mutual interaction of the heart of Christ and the heart of the nun a great spiritual energy was developed which sent lines of power throughout the world. These lines of power touched people who were in spiritual distress and brought them salvation. In one case it would be a sinner on the point of death, his heart rejecting God. The power of the nun's prayer would pierce his heart and at the point of death he would turn to God and be saved. In another case it would be someone struggling with severe temptation and just about to give way to it when the nun's prayer would touch him and renew his strength.

Many such incidents did the old priest see during his moment of supernatural insight, and then the vision faded and the convent chapel was just as before. But he had learnt his lesson and now he felt only admiration and reverence for the figure kneeling before the tabernacle. I relate this incident simply as an illustration of a truth that we know otherwise with the certainty of faith, namely, that our prayers can bring real help to people we do not even know. The closer we are to Christ, the more deeply our spirit is immersed in his, the greater is our power to bring help to others.

The saints are vividly aware of this greatest of all means of helping people. Through their contemplation they were able to live in two worlds at the same time, the material world which they saw around them and the invisible, spiritual world which was also all around them and which they saw by the light of faith. Whatever their work might be in the material world, they did it with an energy inspired by the love they received through contemplation. Their love for people was tireless, showing itself in all kinds of good works. But they knew that the secret of their power lay in contemplation. And they knew that by contemplation itself they could do things for people that no material good works would be able to do.

A fine example of this zeal is shown in the life of St Therese of Lisieux. As a young girl she was attracted to missionary life. Instead she deliberately chose the enclosed life of a Carmelite nun, because she believed that in this way she would help people more. Already in childhood she knew the power of contemplative meditation. Later on as a nun she again felt the attraction of external good works, but no one field of action would be enough for her. She wanted to do everything all at once. She wanted to preach the gospel all over the world. She wanted to be a priest. Above all she wanted to be a martyr. Whatever any of the saints ever did or suffered for Christ, she wanted to do the same. All this sounds naive, immature, unrealistic, but it was not any of these. It was the effect of a mighty love that nothing could satisfy. It was by prayerful reading of the Bible that she found the answer. St Paul describes the Church as the body of Christ, and as the body is composed of different members so in the Church there are different functions: apostles, prophets, teachers, healers etc. No one person can be everything. The eye cannot be the hand as well, nor the ear be the foot.

That should have satisfied her but it did not. She still wanted to be everything. Then reading on she found St Paul explaining that other gifts are of no value without love: it is love that gives meaning to them all. That was her answer. The Church has a heart and that heart is on fire with love. From this heart comes the power that energizes all other activities in the Church. If love ever ceased, these activities would fail and come to nothing. To this her reaction was "I have found my vocation. My vocation is love. In the heart of the Church, my mother, I will be love. Thus I shall be all things at once and satisfy my desires". But Therese was practical; love must be shown by deeds, and this meant living her daily life in a continual spirit of sacrifice. Nothing would be too great, nothing too small to do and to suffer for love of Jesus. The impact she has since made on the world is proof of how right she was.

The great saints are the geniuses of Christianity, and geniuses of any kind are just a small proportion of the general population. But we are all called to be saints according to our individual capacity. Therefore the principles that governed the lives of the great saints must be the principles that govern our lives also. Contemplative meditation leads us into the way of the saints even though we may not be called to live this life with the same intensity as they did. But what it did for them in an exceptional degree it does for us according to the measure of our powers.

It brings us into harmony with God who is the Source of our existence, the guiding Light of all our thoughts and actions, the Power that heals our wounds and gives peace and security to our lives. Above all it gives us love, a love that is strong and deep and pure. We know what it is to have God for our friend, and from this friendship with God there expands a radiance that opens our hearts to other people and wins their love in return. We are loved by many people yet what they love in us is not just ourselves; it is the loveliness of God they see in us.